Other Volumes Available in the *ISMS SERIES:*

BRUNO LEONE received his B.A. (Phi Kappa Phi) from Arizona State University and his M.A. in history from the University of Minnesota. A Woodrow Wilson Fellow (1967) and former instructor at Minneapolis Community College, he has taught history, anthropology, and political science. In 1974-75, he was awarded a Fellowship by the National Endowment for the Humanities to research the intellectual origins of American Democracy. He has edited numerous titles in the *Opposing Viewpoints Series.*

The Isms: Modern Doctrines and Movements

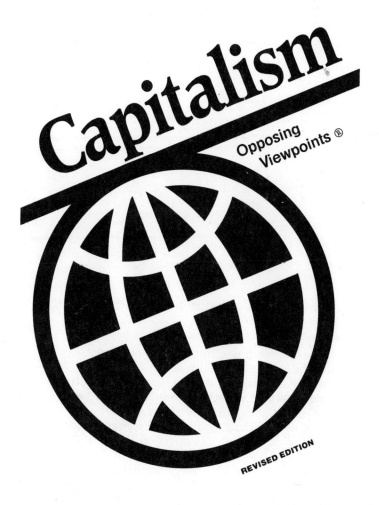

Capitalism

Opposing Viewpoints ®

REVISED EDITION

Bruno Leone

Greenhaven Press
577 Shoreview Park Road
St. Paul, Minnesota 55126

Library of Congress Cataloging-in-Publication Data

Capitalism : opposing viewpoints.

(The Isms : modern doctrines and movements)
Includes bibliographies and index.
Summary: An anthology tracing the key elements of capitalistic theory and practice from Karl Marx to the present. Also includes opposing views on the relationship of capitalism and labor, the strengths and weaknesses of capitalism, its impact on the Third World, and its future.
  1. Capitalism—Addresses, essays, lectures—Juvenile literature. [1. Capitalism—Addresses, essays, lectures]
I. Leone, Bruno, 1939-   . II. Series: Isms.
HB501.C24246 1986   330.12'2   86-3079
ISBN 0-89908-384-6 (lib. bdg.)
ISBN 0-89908-359-5 (pbk.)

Second Edition
Revised

''Congress shall make no law . . .
abridging the freedom of speech,
or of the press.''

first amendment to the U.S. Constitution

The basic foundation of our democracy is the first amendment
guarantee of freedom of expression. The Opposing Viewpoints
books are dedicated to the concept of this basic freedom and the
idea that it is more important to practice it than to enshrine it.

891213

Contents

Why Consider Opposing Viewpoints?

The Importance of Examining Opposing Viewpoints

The purpose of the Opposing Viewpoints books, and this book in particular, is to present balanced, and often difficult to find, opposing points of view on complex and sensitive issues.

Probably the best way to become informed is to analyze the positions of those who are regarded as experts and well studied on issues. It is important to consider every variety of opinion in an attempt to determine the truth. Opinions from the mainstream of society should be examined. But also important are opinions that are considered radical, reactionary, or minority as well as those stigmatized by some other uncomplimentary label. An important lesson of history is the eventual acceptance of many unpopular and even despised opinions. The ideas of Socrates, Jesus, and Galileo are good examples of this.

Readers will approach this book with their own opinions on the issues debated within it. However, to have a good grasp of one's own viewpoint, it is necessary to understand the arguments of those with whom one disagrees. It can be said that those who do not completely understand their adversary's point of view do not fully understand their own.

A persuasive case for considering opposing viewpoints has been presented by John Stuart Mill in his work *On Liberty*. When examining controversial issues it may be helpful to reflect on this suggestion:

> The only way in which a human being can make some approach to knowing the whole of a subject, is by hearing what can be said about it by persons of every variety of opinion, and studying all modes in which it can be looked at by every character of mind. No wise man ever acquired his wisdom in any mode but this.

Analyzing Sources of Information

The Opposing Viewpoints books include diverse materials taken from magazines, journals, books, and newspapers, as well as statements and position papers from a wide range of individuals, organizations and governments. This broad spectrum of sources helps to develop patterns of thinking which are open to the consideration of a variety of opinions.

Pitfalls to Avoid

A pitfall to avoid in considering opposing points of view is that of regarding one's own opinion as being common sense and the most rational stance and the point of view of others as being only opinion and naturally wrong. It may be that another's opinion is correct and one's own is in error.

Another pitfall to avoid is that of closing one's mind to the opinions of those with whom one disagrees. The best way to approach a dialogue is to make one's primary purpose that of understanding the mind and arguments of the other person and not that of enlightening him or her with one's own solutions. More can be learned by listening than speaking.

It is my hope that after reading this book the reader will have a deeper understanding of the issues debated and will appreciate the complexity of even seemingly simple issues on which good and honest people disagree. This awareness is particularly important in a democratic society such as ours where people enter into public debate to determine the common good. Those with whom one disagrees should not necessarily be regarded as enemies, but perhaps simply as people who suggest different paths to a common goal.

Developing Basic Reading and Thinking Skills

In this book carefully edited opposing viewpoints are purposely placed back to back to create a running debate; each viewpoint is preceded by a short quotation that best expresses the author's main argument. This format instantly plunges the reader into the midst of a controversial issue and greatly aids that reader in mastering the basic skill of recognizing an author's point of view.

A number of basic skills for critical thinking are practiced in the activities that appear throughout the books in the series. Some of the skills are:

Evaluating Sources of Information   The ability to choose from among alternative sources the most reliable and accurate source in relation to a given subject.

Separating Fact from Opinion   The ability to make the basic distinction between factual statements (those that can be demonstrated or verified empirically) and statements of opinion (those that are beliefs or attitudes that cannot be proved).

Identifying Stereotypes   The ability to identify oversimplified, exaggerated descriptions (favorable or unfavorable) about people and insulting statements about racial, religious or national groups, based upon misinformation or lack of information.

Recognizing Ethnocentrism   The ability to recognize attitudes or opinions that express the view that one's own race, culture, or group is inherently superior, or those attitudes that judge another culture or group in terms of one's own.

It is important to consider opposing viewpoints and equally important to be able to critically analyze those viewpoints. The activities in this book are designed to help the reader master these thinking skills. Statements are taken from the book's viewpoints and the reader is asked to analyze them. This technique aids the reader in developing skills that not only can be applied to the viewpoints in this book, but also to situations where opinionated spokespersons comment on controversial issues. Although the activities are helpful to the solitary reader, they are most useful when the reader can benefit from the interaction of group discussion.

Using this book and others in the series should help readers develop basic reading and thinking skills. These skills should improve the readers' ability to understand what they read. Readers should be better able to separate fact from opinion, substance from rhetoric and become better consumers of information in our media-centered culture.

This volume of the Opposing Viewpoints books does not advocate a particular point of view. Quite the contrary! The very nature of the book leaves it to the reader to formulate the opinions he or she finds most suitable. My purpose as publisher is to see that this is made possible by offering a wide range of viewpoints which are fairly presented.

David L. Bender
Publisher

Preface to
First Edition

In its broadest sense, capitalism is an economic principle which probably predates recorded history. As long as a demand has existed for goods and services and individuals have been available to satisfy that demand at a personal profit, capitalism may be said to have existed. It was not until the eighteenth and nineteenth centuries in Europe that modern capitalism was born. It grew out of a series of philosophical, technological, and economic developments which combined to give rise to modern industry and its accompanying market system. (Historians refer to the period as the Industrial Revolution.)

Popularly known as the "free-enterprise system," modern capitalism is distinguished from its economic predecessors by certain features which include: the private and corporate ownership of factories and other production facilities; a system of markets in which individuals and corporations purchase and sell goods and services; a labor force legally free to choose any available avenue of employment; the sale of labor for money; the universal use of money for the purchase of goods; and the growth of technology.

Previously, the absence of machinery restricted the amount of goods produced which, in turn, placed limitations upon the economic system. However, during the Industrial Revolution, the hand labors of artisans and their apprentices, private barter, and other modes of production and economic exchange disappeared or became quaint remnants of days past. In their place, mechanized industries began spreading throughout Western Europe, America, and eventually the entire world. Along with this change, free and competitive markets replaced governmental regulation of national economies.

The new system was met with extreme reactions. It was hailed as a boon by some and condemned as a monster by others. To the good, it was argued that capitalism was creating an abundance of jobs by greatly expanding the productive market. Along with the market, national economies were growing at an unprecedented rate. And finally, both the quantity and quality of goods available for public consumption were experiencing a significant improvement. To the bad, a sympathetic finger was pointed at the unfortunate worker, one of the primary architects of this fabulous new economic structure. Men, women, and children were required to labor excessively long hours, often in unsafe and bestial surroundings, for a bare, subsistence wage. The gap between rich and poor (owner and worker) increased as rapidly as industry grew. However significant were the economic achievements of capitalism, socially, opponents said, it was a depressing moral failure.

The following chapters explore the evolution of this controversy. The viewpoints offer both the theoretical and practical positions for and against capitalism. However, the reader is asked to note that while the arguments have continually changed to suit contemporary circumstances, their tone remains consistently passionate.

Preface to Second Edition

It is with pleasure and an enormous degree of satisfaction that the second edition of Greenhaven Press's *ISMS Series: Opposing Viewpoints* has been published. The Series was so well received when it initially was made available in 1978 that plans for its revision were almost immediately formulated. During the following years, the enthusiasm of librarians and classroom teachers provided the editor with the necessary encouragement to complete the project.

While the Opposing Viewpoints format of the series has remained the same, each of the books has undergone a major revision. Because the series is developed along historical lines, materials were added or deleted in the opening chapters only where historical interpretations have changed or new sources were uncovered. The final chapters of each book have been comprehensively recast to reflect changes in the national and international situations since the original titles were published.

The Series began with six titles: *Capitalism, Communism, Internationalism, Nationalism, Racism,* and *Socialism.* A new and long overdue title, *Feminism,* has been added and several additional ones are being considered for the future. The editor offers his deepest gratitude to the dedicated and talented editorial staff of Greenhaven Press for its countless and invaluable contributions. A special thanks goes to Bonnie Szumski, whose gentle encouragement and indomitable aplomb helped carry the developing manuscripts over many inevitable obstacles. Finally, the editor thanks all future readers and hopes that the 1986 edition of the *ISMS Series* will enjoy the same reception as its predecessor.

The Theory and Practice of Capitalism

Introduction

One of the first and most persuasive advocates of modern capitalism was Adam Smith. A Scotsman, Smith became (and still remains) the prophet of the new economic order. In his epochal work, *The Wealth of Nations*, he provided a compelling and all-inclusive rationale for the capitalistic system. It is to his credit that contemporary defenders of the principle parrot his basic arguments virtually unchanged.

The fundamental theme of *The Wealth of Nations* is what Smith's later supporters termed the doctrine of laissez-faire ("hands-off") capitalism. The doctrine held that the world of economics functions under "natural laws" which operate exclusive of politics. Government intervention in the economic order of things will upset these "natural laws" and thereby disrupt a nation's economy. However, by maintaining a "hands-off" policy and allowing private citizens complete economic freedom, governments can ensure the growth of a nation's wealth.

Smith realized that under a free enterprise system, individuals would pursue their own self-interests. Anticipating his critics, Smith contended, however, that self-serving individuals, with the help of an "invisible hand" (i.e. competition), would be contributing to the welfare of all. In other words, in order to build and maintain a flourishing and profitable concern, a businessman's products would have to be needed, well made, and competitively priced. If not, he would be unable to compete successfully with others also pursuing their self-interests. Morever, he would be creating jobs and helping to expand the general economy. Thus the "natural laws" of economics, when unrestrained, would profit not only industry but government and labor as well.

The most serious challenge to Adam Smith and his followers came from Karl Marx, a nineteenth-century German. The son of a Prussian lawyer, the methodical Marx proved a worthy and resourceful opponent. He unfolded his economic theories in his monumental *Das Kapital* (Capital), a work on which he spent eighteen years researching and writing.

Marx's primary objection to the capitalistic system was that it was grossly unfair to the worker. To illustrate this, he developed his now famous theory of "surplus values." The theory involves the intricate relationship between the worker and his product and the employer and his profit. In effect, Marx was saying that the worker received as salary only a small part of the value of the good produced. The difference between the cost of labor and the price at which a product was sold constituted the employer's profit. Hence, "surplus value" represented that monetary portion of a product for which a worker toiled but received no pay. In brief, the theory implied that whatever profits the capitalist class acquired, it stole from the workers.

Marx's solution to this exploitative situation was a simple one. The means of production and exchange should be taken from the capitalists and turned over to the workers. This would eliminate the problem of "surplus value," since the working class would be producing and exchanging goods for itself as a collective unit.

Since Smith and Marx voiced their respective theories, the world of capital and labor has undergone numerous substantive changes. These changes have been the result of far-reaching transformations in the political, social, technological, and economic patterns governing the world of the nineteenth and twentieth centuries. However, many of the theoretical and practical arguments supporting or condemning capitalism have remained faithful to the spirit of Smith and Marx. The viewpoints by Lloyd, Rockefeller, von Mises, and Marcuse illustrate this and underline the enormous influence of the two earlier theorists.

"Every man, as long as he does not violate the laws of justice, is left perfectly free to pursue his own interest his own way."

Free Enterprise Is the Key to a Prosperous Society

Adam Smith

Adam Smith, a political economist, was born in Scotland. He was educated at the universities of Glasgow and Oxford and later taught English literature, economics, logic and moral philosophy at Glasgow University. In 1776, Smith published *The Wealth of Nations*. Systematic, comprehensive, and forceful, the work was an immediate success and became widely recognized by businessmen and statesmen as the authoritative statement on political economy. In the following viewpoint, Smith explains why individual "self-interest" is beneficial to society as a whole and why governmental intervention in business retards "the progress of society towards real wealth and greatness."

As you read, consider the following questions:

1. How does the author believe self-interest benefits society?
2. According to the author, of what value is the profit motive?
3. Why does the author argue that the government retards progress?

Adam Smith, *The Wealth of Nations*, New York: Random House, 1965.

The general industry of the society never can exceed what the capital of the society can employ. As the number of workmen that can be kept in employment by any particular person must bear a certain proportion to his capital, so the number of those that can be continually employed by all the members of a great society, must bear a certain proportion to the whole capital of that society, and never can exceed that proportion. No regulation of commerce can increase the quantity of industry in any society beyond what its capital can maintain. It can only divert a part of it into a direction into which it might not otherwise have gone; and it is by no means certain that this artificial direction is likely to be more advantageous to the society than that into which it would have gone of its own accord.

Self-Interest Benefits Society

Every individual is continually exerting himself to find out the most advantageous employment for whatever capital he can command. It is his own advantage, indeed, and not that of the society, which he has in view. But the study of his own advantage naturally, or rather necessarily leads him to prefer that employment which is most advantageous to the society.

First, every individual endeavors to employ his capital as near home as he can, and consequently as much as he can in the support of domestic industry; provided always that he can thereby obtain the ordinary...profits....

The Profit Motive

Secondly, every individual who employs his capital in the support of domestic industry, necessarily endeavours so to direct that industry, that its produce may be of the greatest possible value.

The produce of industry is what it adds to the subject or materials upon which it is employed. In proportion as the value of this produce is great or small, so will likewise be the profits of the employer. But it is only for the sake of profit that any man employs a capital in the support of industry; and he will always, therefore, endeavour to employ it in the support of that industry of which the produce is likely to be of the greatest value, or to exchange for the greatest quantity either of money or of other goods.

The "Invisible Hand" and Society

But the annual revenue of every society is always precisely equal to the exchangeable value of the whole annual produce of its industry, or rather is precisely the same thing with that exchangeable value. As every individual, therefore, endeavours as much as he can both to employ his capital in the support of domestic industry, and so to direct that industry that its produce may be of the greatest value; every individual necessarily labours to render the annual revenue of the society as great as he can. He generally, indeed, neither intends to promote the public interest, nor knows how much he is promoting it. By preferring the support of domestic to that of foreign industry, he intends only his own security; and by directing that industry in such a manner as its produce may be of the greatest value, he intends only his own gain, and he is in this, as in many other cases, led by an invisible hand to promote an end which was no part of his intention. Nor is it always the worse for the society that it was no part of it. By pursuing his own interest he frequently promotes that of the society more effectually than when he really intends to promote it. I have never known much good done by those who affected to trade for the public good....

The Superior Judgment of the Capitalist

What is the species of domestic industry which his capital can employ, and of which the produce is likely to be of the greatest value, every individual, it is evident, can, in his local situation, judge much better than any statesman or lawgiver can do for him. The statesman, who should attempt to direct private people in what manner they ought to employ their capitals, would not only load himself with a most unnecessary attention, but assume an authority which could safely be trusted, not only to no single person, but to no council or senate whatever, and which would nowhere be so dangerous as in the hands of a man who had folly and presumption enough to fancy himself fit to exercise it....

What Is Capital?

Capital is that part of the wealth of a country which is employed in production, and consists of food, clothing, tools, raw materials, machinery, etc., necessary to give effect to labour.

David Ricardo, *Principles of Political Economy and Taxation.*

It is thus that every system which endeavours, either, by extraordinary encouragements, to draw towards a particular species of industry a greater share of the capital of the society than what would naturally go to it; or, by extraordinary restraints, to force from a particular species of industry some share of the capital which would otherwise be employed in it; is in reality subversive of the great purpose which it means to promote. It retards, instead of accelerating, the progress of the society towards real wealth and greatness; and diminishes, instead of increasing, the real value of the annual produce of its land and labour....

Every man, as long as he does not violate the laws of justice, is left perfectly free to pursue his own interest his own way, and to bring both his industry and capital into competition with those of any other man, or order of men. The sovereign [government] is completely discharged from a duty, in the attempting to perform which he must always be exposed to innumerable delusions, and for the proper performance of which no human wisdom or knowledge could ever be sufficient; the duty of superintending the industry of private people, and of directing it towards the employments most suitable to the interest of the society. According to the system of natural liberty, the sovereign has only three duties to attend to; three duties of great importance, indeed, but plain and intelligible to common understandings: first, the duty of protecting the society from the violence and invasion of other independent societies; secondly, the duty of protecting, as far as possible, every member of the society from the injustice or oppression of every other member of it, or the duty of establishing an exact administration of justice; and, thirdly, the duty of erecting and maintaining certain public works and certain public institutions, which it can never be for the interest of any individual, or small number of individuals, to erect and maintain; because the profit could never repay the expence to any individual or small number of individuals, though it may frequently do much more than repay it to a great society.

"Modern industry has converted the little workshop of the patriarchal master into the great factory of the industrial capitalist."

Free Enterprise Demoralizes Society

Karl Marx

Karl Marx is considered to be the founder of modern scientific socialism. Educated in Germany at the Universities of Bonn, Berlin, and Jena, Marx turned to communism while in Paris as a result of further studies in philosophy, history, and political science. In 1844, he met Friedrich Engels, with whom he collaborated to systematize the theoritical principles of communism. Although his influence was small during his lifetime, it grew enormously with the spread of socialism and the growth of the labor movement. The following viewpoint, excerpted from *The Manifesto of the Communist Party*, was written by Marx on the basis of a draft prepared by Engels. The excerpt includes some of the fundamental concepts of communism.

As you read, consider the following questions:

1. The author believes that society can be divided into two classes. What are they?
2. In what ways does the author believe the workers are exploited?
3. What, according to the author, is the role of the proletariat?
4. What should the ultimate aim of communism be, according to Marx?

Karl Marx and Friedrich Engels, *The Manifesto of the Communist Party*, Peking: Foreign Language Press, 1970.

The history of all hitherto existing society is the history of class struggles.

Our epoch, the epoch of the bourgeoisie, possesses, however, this distinctive feature: it has simplified the class antagonisms. Society as a whole is more and more splitting up into two great hostile camps, into two great classes directly facing each other: Bourgeoisie and Proletariat*....

The bourgeoisie has, since the establishment of Modern Industry and of the world market, conquered for itself, in the modern representative State, exclusive political sway. The executive of the modern State is but a committee for managing the common affairs of the whole bourgeoisie.

Bourgeois Excesses

The bourgeoisie, historically, has played a most revolutionary part.

The bourgeoisie, wherever it has got the upper hand, has put an end to all feudal, patriarchal, idyllic relations. It has pitilessly torn asunder the motley feudal ties that bound man to his "natural superiors," and has left remaining no other nexus between man and man than naked self-interest, than callous "cash payment." It has drowned the most heavenly ecstasies of religious fervour, of chivalrous enthusiasm, of philistine sentimentalism, in the icy water of egotistical calculation. It has resolved personal worth into exchange value, and in place of the numberless indefeasible chartered freedoms, has set up that single, unconscionable freedom—Free Trade. In one word, for exploitation, veiled by religious and political illusions, it has substituted naked, shameless, direct, brutal exploitation.

The bourgeoisie has stripped of its halo every occupation hitherto honoured and looked up to with reverent awe. It has converted the physician, the lawyer, the priest, the poet, the man of science, into its paid wage-labourers.

The bourgeoisie has torn away from the family its sentimental veil, and has reduced the family relation to a mere money relation....

The conditions of bourgeois society are too narrow to comprise the wealth created by them. And how does the bourgeoisie get over [this]? On the one hand by enforced destruction of a mass of productive forces; on the other, by the conquest of new markets, and by the more thorough exploitation of the old ones. That is to say, by paving the way for more extensive and more destructive crises, and by diminishing the means whereby crises are prevented.

The weapons with which the bourgeoisie felled feudalism [its

*By bourgeoisie is meant the class of modern Capitalists, owners of the means of social production and employers of wage-labour. By proletariat, the class of modern wage-labourers who, having no means of production of their own, are reduced to selling their labour-power in order to live. [Note by Engels to the English edition of 1888.]

25

predecessor] to the ground are now turned against the bourgeoisie itself.

But not only has the bourgeoisie forged the weapons that bring death to itself; it has also called into existence the men who are to wield those weapons—the modern working class—the proletarians.

The Role of the Proletariat

In proportion as the bourgeoisie, *i.e.*, capital, is developed, in the same proportion is the proletariat, the modern working class, developed—a class of labourers, who live only so long as they find work, and who find work only so long as their labour increases capital. These labourers, who must sell themselves piecemeal, are a commodity, like every other article of commerce, and are consequently exposed to all the vicissitudes of competition, to all the fluctuations of the market.

Capitalism Is Self-Destructive

Capitalism did not arise because capitalists stole the land or the workmen's tools, but because it was more efficient than feudalism. It will perish because it is not merely less efficient than socialism, but actually self-destructive.

J.B.S. Haldane, *I Believe.*

Owing to the extensive use of machinery and to division of labour, the work of the proletarians has lost all individual character, and, consequently, all charm for the workman. He becomes an appendage of the machine, and it is only the most simple, most monotonous, and most easily acquired knack, that is required of him. Hence, the cost of production of a workman is restricted, almost entirely, to the means of subsistence that he requires for his maintenance, and for the propagation of his race. But the price of a commodity, and therefore also of labour, is equal to its cost of production. In proportion, therefore, as the repulsiveness of the work increases, the wage decreases. Nay more, in proportion as the use of machinery and division of labour increases, in the same proportion the burden of toil also increases, whether by prolongation of the working hours, by increase of the work exacted in a given time or by increased speed of the machinery, etc.

The Exploitation of the Worker

Modern industry has converted the little workshop of the patriarchal master into the great factory of the industrial capitalist. Masses of labourers, crowded into the factory, are organised like soldiers. As privates of the industrial army they are placed under the command of a perfect hierarchy of officers and sergeants. Not only are

Karl Marx

they slaves of the bourgeois class, and of the bourgeois State; they are daily and hourly enslaved by the machine, by the overlookers, and, above all, by the individual bourgeois manufacturer himself. The more openly this despotism proclaims gain to be its end and aim, the more petty, the more hateful and the more embittering it is.

The less the skill and exertion of strength implied in manual labour, in other words, the more modern industry becomes developed, the more is the labour of men superseded by that of women. Differences of age and sex have no longer any distinctive social validity for the working class. All are instruments of labour, more or less expensive to use, according to their age and sex.

No sooner is the exploitation of the labourer by the manufacturer, so far, at an end, that he receives his wages in cash, than he is set upon by the other portions of the bourgeoisie, the landlord, the shopkeeper, the pawnbroker, etc....

The Bourgeoisie: Its Own Grave-Digger

The essential condition for the existence, and for the sway of the bourgeois class, is the formation and augmentation of capital; the condition for capital is wage-labour. Wage-labour rests exclusively on competition between the labourers. The advance of industry, whose involuntary promoter is the bourgeoisie, replaces the isolation of the labourers, due to competition, by their revolutionary combination, due to association. The development of Modern Industry, therefore, cuts from under its feet the very foundation on which the bourgeoisie produces and appropriates products. What the bourgeoisie, therefore, produces, above all, are its own grave-diggers. Its fall and the victory of the proletariat are equally inevitable....

The Aim of Communism

The immediate aim of the Communists is the same as that of all the other proletarian parties: formation of the proletariat into a class, overthrow of the bourgeois supremacy, conquest of political power by the proletariat....

The Communists disdain to conceal their views and aims. They openly declare that their ends can be attained only by the forcible overthrow of all existing social conditions. Let the ruling classes tremble at a Communistic revolution. The proletarians have nothing to lose but their chains. They have a world to win.

Working Men of All Countries, Unite!

"We have given competition its own way, and have found that we are not good enough or wise enough to be trusted with this power."

Free Enterprise Should Be Regulated

Henry Demarest Lloyd

Henry Demarest Lloyd was an American journalist and reformer. His famous book, *Wealth Against Commonwealth*, is an attack on monopolies in general, and the Standard Oil Company is particular. Lloyd did more than just attack capitalistic practices. Through his writings, he ardently campaigned on a number of issues from populism to socialism. In the following viewpoint, Lloyd attacks the "lords of industry," claiming they ruthlessly rape and plunder society in order to attain riches for themselves. He calls for more federal regulation as a means to moderate the excesses of big business.

As you read, consider the following questions:

1. What example does Lloyd give to show how large companies work against the average man?
2. What is missing from society, according to the author?

Henry Demarest Lloyd, *The Lords of Industry*. New York: G.P. Putnam's Sons, 1910.

Adam Smith said in 1776: "People of the same trade hardly meet together even for merriment and diversion but the conversation ends in a conspiracy against the public or in some contrivance to raise prices." The expansive ferment of the New Industry, coming with the new science, the new land, and the new liberties of our era, broke up these "conspiracies," and for a century we have heard nothing of them; but the race to overrun is being succeeded by the struggle to divide, and combinations are re-appearing on all sides. This any one may see from the reports of the proceedings of the conventions and meetings of innumerable associations of manufacturers and dealers and even producers, which are being held almost constantly. They all do something to raise prices, or hold them up, and they wind up with banquets for which we pay....

"A Binding Arrangement"

Last July Messrs. [Cornelius] Vanderbilt, [Samuel] Sloan, and one or two others out of several hundred owners of coal lands and coal railroads, met in the pleasant shadows of Saratoga to make "a binding arrangement for the control of the coal trade." "Binding arrangement" the sensitive coal presidents say they prefer to the word "combination." The gratuitous warmth of summer suggested to these men the need the public would have of artificial heat, at artificial prices, the coming winter. It was agreed to fix prices, and to prevent the production of too much of the raw material of warmth, by suspensions of mining. In anticipation of the arrival of the cold-wave from Manitoba, a cold wave was sent out all over the United States, from their parlors in New York, in an order for half-time work by the miners during the first three months of this year, and for an increase of prices. These are the means this combination uses to keep down wages—the price of men, and keep up the price of coal—the wages of capital....

There has been since 1872 a national combination of the manufacturers of the stoves, into which the combination coal must be put; and its effect, the founder said, in his speech at the annual banquet in Cleveland, last February, had been to change the balance from the wrong to the right side of the ledger. Until lately, at least, combination matches lighted the fire of combination coal in these combination stoves and it is combination oil which the cook, contrary to orders, puts on the fires to make them burn faster. The combination of match manufacturers was perfected by the experience of sixteen years of fusions, till lately it shared with the coal combination the pleasure of advancing the price of fire by proclamation on the approach of winter....

Such are some of the pools into which our industry is eddying. They come and go, and those that stay grow. All are "voluntary," of course, but if the milk farmer of Orange county, the iron molder of Troy, the lumber dealer of San Francisco, the Lackawanna Railroad, or any other individual or corporate producer, show any backwardness about accepting the invitation to join "the pool," they are whipped in with all the competitive weapons at command, from assault and battery to boycotting and conspiracy. The private wars that are ravaging our world of trade give small men their choice between extermination and vassalage. Combine or die!...

Pooling the Profits

In a society which has the wherewithal to cover, fatten and cheer every one, Lords of Industry are acquiring the power to pool the profits of scarcity and to decree famine. They cannot stop the brook that runs the mill, but they can chain the wheel; they cannot hide the coal mine, but they can close the shaft three days every week. To keep up gold-digging rates of dividends, they declare war against plenty. On all that keeps him alive the workman must pay them their prices, while they lock him out of the mill in which alone his labor can be made to fetch the price of life. Only society can compel a social use of its resources; the man is for himself.

Dangerous Monopolies

There is more danger from monopolies than from combinations of workingmen. There is more danger that capitalism will swallow up the profits of labor than that labor will confiscate capital.

George Bancroft, October 22, 1834.

On the theory of "too much of everything" our industries, from railroads to workingmen, are being organized to prevent milk, nails, lumber, freights, labor, soothing syrup, and all these other things, from becoming too cheap. The majority have never yet been able to buy enough of anything. The minority have too much of everything to sell. Seeds of social trouble germinate fast in such conditions....

Morality Should Be Society's Focus

We have given competition its own way, and have found that we are not good enough or wise enough to be trusted with this power of ruining ourselves in the attempt to ruin others. Free competition could be let run only in a community where every one had learned to say and act "I am the state." We have had an era of material inventions. We now need a renaissance of moral inventions, contrivances to tap the vast currents of moral magnetism flowing uncaught over the face of society. Morals and values rise and fall together. If our combinations have no morals, they can have no values. If the tendency to combination is irresistible, control of it is imperative. Monopoly and anti-monopoly, odious as these words have become to the literary ear, represent the two great tendencies of our time: monopoly, the tendency to combination; anti-monopoly, the demand for social control of it. As the man is bent toward business or patriotism, he will negotiate combinations or agitate for laws to regulate them. The first is capitalistic, the second is social. The first, industrial; the second, moral. The first promotes wealth; the second, citizenship. These combinations are not to be waved away as fresh pictures of folly or total depravity. There is something in them deeper than that. The Aryan has proved by the experience of thousands of years that he can travel. "But travel," Emerson says, "is the fool's paradise." We must now prove that we can stay at home, and stand it as well as the Chinese have done. Future Puritans cannot emigrate from Southhampton to Plymouth Rock. They can only sail from righteousness to righteousness. Our young men can no longer go west; they must go up or down. Not new land, but new virtue must be the outlet for the future. Our halt at the shores of the Pacific is a much more serious affair than that which brought our ancestors to a pause before the barriers of the Atlantic, and compelled them to practice living together for a few hundred years. We cannot hereafter, as in the past, recover freedom by going to the prairies; we must find it in the society of the good. In the presence of great combinations, in all departments of life, the moralist and patriot have work to do of a significance never before approached during the itinerant phases of our civilization. It may be that the coming age of combination will issue in a nobler and fuller liberty for the individual than has yet been seen, but that consummation will be possible, not in a day of competitive trade, but in one of competitive morals.

"I ascribe the success of the Standard to its consistent policy to make the volume of its business large through the merits and cheapness of its products."

Free Enterprise Should Not Be Regulated

John D. Rockefeller

John David Rockefeller was a prominent industrialist and philanthropist. Through a combination of frugality, ruthlessness and keen business sense, Rockefeller managed to make his Standard Oil Company one of the largest and most powerful corporations in the nation. Rockefeller held a virtual monopoly on the production of oil through a huge network of refineries, oil and rail lines, and retail outlets. After the enactment of the Sherman Anti-Trust Act of 1890, Rockefeller was twice found in violation of the act and forced to relinquish subsidiary holdings. Rockefeller was also a generous philanthropist and was responsible for founding many institutions that survive him, including the University of Chicago. In the following viewpoint, excerpted from testimony before a governmental investigating body, Rockefeller argues that unregulated business provides higher wages for employees.

As you read, consider the following questions:

1. What advantages does Rockefeller believe are derived from huge combinations of companies?
2. Compare Rockefeller's ideas to the consequences of the breakup of AT&T. Do you think Rockefeller was right that huge companies provide better service?

Q: To what advantages, or favors, or methods of management do you ascribe chiefly the success of the Standard Oil Company?

A: I ascribe the success of the Standard to its consistent policy to make the volume of its business large through the merits and cheapness of its products. It has spared no expense in finding, securing, and utilizing the best and cheapest methods of manufacture. It has sought for the best superintendents and workmen and paid the best wages. It has not hesitated to sacrifice old machinery and old plants for new and better ones. It has placed its manufactories at the points where they could supply markets at the least expense. It has not only sought markets for its principal products, but for all possible by-products, sparing no expense in introducing them to the public. It has not hesitated to invest millions of dollars in methods of cheapening the gathering and distribution of oils by pipe lines, special cars, tank steamers, and tank wagons. It has erected tank stations at every important railroad station to cheapen the storage and delivery of its products. It has spared no expense in forcing its products into the markets of the world among people civilized and uncivilized. It has had faith in American oil, and has brought together millions of money for the purpose of making it what it is, and holding its markets against the competition of Russia and all the many countries which are producers of oil....

Formation of Corporations a Necessity

Q: What are, in your judgment, the chief advantages from industrial combinations—(a) financially to stockholders; (b) to the public?

A: All the advantages which can be derived from a cooperation of persons and aggregation of capital....Two persons in partnership may be a sufficiently large combination for a small business, but if the business grows or can be made to grow, more persons and more capital must be taken in. The business may grow so large that a partnership ceases to be a proper instrumentality for its purposes, and then a corporation becomes a necessity....Our Federal form of government, making every corporation created by a state foreign to every other state, renders it necessary for persons doing business through corporate agency to organize corporations in some or many of the different states in which their business is located. Instead of doing business through the agency of one corporation they must do business through the agencies of several corporations. If the business is extended to foreign countries, and Americans are not today satisfied with home markets alone, it will be found helpful and possibly necessary to organize corporations in such countries, for Europeans are prejudiced against foreign corporations as are the people of many of our states....

It is too late to argue about advantages of industrial combinations. They are a necessity....Their chief advantages are:

(1) Command of necessary capital.

34

(2) Extension of limits of business.

(3) Increase of number of persons interested in the business.

(4) Economy in the business.

(5) Improvements and economies which are derived from knowledge of many interested persons of wide experience.

(6) Power to give the public improved products at less prices and still make a profit for stockholders.

(7) Permanent work and good wages for laborers.

Voice of Experience

I speak from my experience in the business with which I have been intimately connected for about forty years. Our first combination was a partnership and afterward a corporation in Ohio. That was sufficient for a local refining business. But dependent solely upon local business we should have failed years ago. We were forced to extend our markets and to seek for export trade. This latter made the seaboard cities a necessary place of business, and we soon discovered that manufacturing for export could be more economically carried on at the seaboard, hence refineries at Brooklyn, at Bayonne, at Philadelphia, and necessary corporations in New York, New Jersey, and Pennsylvania.

We soon discovered as the business grew that the primary method of transporting oil in barrels could not last. The package often cost more than the contents, and the forests of the country were not sufficient to supply the necessary material for an extended length of time. Hence we...adopted the pipe-line system, and found capital for pipe-line construction equal to the necessities of the business.

No More Demoralizing Theory

There is no more demoralizing theory than that which imputes all human evils to Capitalism or any other single agency.

Samuel Gompers, *Seventy Years of Life and Labor,* 1925.

To operate pipe-lines required franchises from the states in which they were located, and consequently corporations in those states, just as railroads running through different states are forced to operate under separate state charters. To perfect the pipe-line system of transportation required in the neighborhood of fifty millions of capital. This could not be obtained or maintained without industrial combination. The entire oil business is dependent upon its pipe-line system. Without it every well would shut down and every foreign market would be closed to us.

The pipe-line system required other improvements, such as tank cars upon railways, and finally the tank steamer. Capital had to be furnished for them and corporations created to own and operate them.

Every step taken was necessary in the business if it was to be properly developed, and only through such successive steps and by such an industrial combination is America today enabled to utilize the bounty which its land pours forth, and to furnish the world with the best and cheapest light ever known, receiving in return therefor from foreign lands nearly $50,000,000 per year, most of which is distributed in payment of American labor.

I have given a picture rather than a detail of the growth of one industrial combination. It is a pioneer, and its work has been of incalculable value. There are other American products besides oil for which the markets of the world can be opened, and legislators will be blind to our best industrial interests if they unduly hinder by legislation the combination of persons and capital requisite for the attainment of so desirable an end.

"Capitalism has poured a horn of plenty upon the masses of the wage earners who...did all they could to sabotage the adoption of those innovations which render life more agreeable."

Capitalism Guarantees Human Freedom

Ludwig von Mises

Ludwig von Mises was a prominent economist and one of the first to believe that economics should be treated as a rational science. Born and educated in Austria, he received a doctorate in Canon and Roman Law from the University of Vienna in 1906. Von Mises was professor of economics at the University of Vienna, and founded the Austrian Institute of Business Psycho Research where he served as vice president from 1926 to 1938. He immigrated to the US in 1940, and resumed his teaching career in 1945 as a professor of economics at New York University. In addition to teaching, von Mises also authored several books, including *Planning for Freedom, The Anti-Capitalist Mentality,* and *The Ultimate Foundation of Economic Science.* In the following viewpoint, excerpted from his book *Human Action,* Mr. von Mises comments on several common objections to capitalism.

As you read, consider the following questions:

1. How, according to the author, does the Soviet economy imitate that of the US?
2. Why, according to von Mises, is profit a positive thing in the economy?
3. What is wrong with socialism, according to the author?

Reprinted from *Human Action* © 1949 by Ludwig von Mises, used with permission of Contemporary Books, Inc., Chicago.

On Capitalism

The system of free enterprise has been dubbed capitalism in order to deprecate and to smear it. However, this term can be considered very pertinent. It refers to the most characteristic feature of the system, its main eminence, viz., the role the notion of capital plays in its conduct.

Modern capitalism is essentially mass production for the needs of the masses. The buyers of the products are by and large the same people who as wage earners cooperate in their manufacturing.

Capitalism, says Marx, repeating the fables of the eulogists of the Middle Ages, has an inevitable tendency to impoverish the workers more and more. The truth is that capitalism has poured a horn of plenty upon the masses of the wage earners who frequently did all they could to sabotage the adoption of those innovations which render life more agreeable. It is not labor legislation and labor-union pressure that have shortened hours of work and withdrawn married women and children from the factories; it is capitalism.

The history of capitalism as it has operated in the last two hundred years in the realm of Western civilization is the record of a steady rise in the wage earners' standard of living. The inherent mark of capitalism is that it is mass production for mass consumption directed by the most energetic and far-sighted individuals, unflaggingly aiming at improvement. Its driving force is the profit motive, the instrumentality of which forces the businessman constantly to provide the consumers with more, better and cheaper amenities. An excess of profits over losses can appear only in a progressing economy and only to the extent to which the masses' standard of living improves. Thus capitalism is the system under which the keenest and most agile minds are driven to promote the welfare of the laggard many.

Government-operated enterprises and the Russian Soviet economy are, by the mere fact that they buy and sell on markets, connected with the capitalist system. They themselves bear witness to this connection by calculating in terms of money. They thus utilize the intellectual methods of the capitalist system that they fanatically condemn....

On Profit and Loss

Profits are the driving force of the market economy. The greater the profits, the better the needs of the consumers are supplied. For profits can only be reaped by removing discrepancies between the demands of the consumers and the previous state of production activities. He who serves the public best, makes the highest profits. In fighting profits governments deliberately sabotage the operation of the market economy.

The profits of those who have produced goods and services for which the buyers scramble are not the source of the losses of those who have brought to the market commodities in the purchase of which the public is not prepared to pay the full amount of production costs expanded. These losses are caused by the lack of insight displayed in anticipating the future state of the market and the demand of the consumers....

If profits were to be curtailed for the benefit of those whom a change in the data has injured, the adjustment of supply to demand would not be improved but impaired. If one were to prevent doctors from occasionally earning high fees, one would not increase but rather decrease the number of those choosing the medical profession.

An Honest Man

I do not want my attitude to be misunderstood. I shall be glad to state it for the record....I work for nothing but my own profit—which I make by selling a product they need to men who are willing and able to buy it. I do not produce it for their benefit at the expense of mine, and they do not buy it for my benefit at the expense of theirs; I do not sacrifice my interests to them nor do they sacrifice theirs to me; we deal as equals by mutual consent to mutual advantage—and I am proud of every penny that I have earned in this manner. I am rich and I am proud of every penny I own. I have made my money by my own effort, in free exchange and through the voluntary consent of every man I dealt with—the voluntary consent of those who employed me when I started, the voluntary consent of those who work for me now, the voluntary consent of those who buy my product. I shall answer all the questions you are afraid to ask me openly. Do I wish to pay my workers more than their services are worth to me? I do not. Do I wish to sell my product for less than my customers are willing to pay me? I do not. Do I wish to sell it at a loss or give it away? I do not. If this is evil, do whatever you please about me, according to whatever standards you hold. These are mine. I am earning my own living, as every honest man must.

Hank Reardon, in *Altas Shrugged*, by Ayn Rand, 1975.

Profit and loss are favorable to some members of society and unfavorable to others. Hence, people concluded, *the gain of one man is the damage of another; no man profits but by the loss of others.* This dogma is at the bottom of all modern doctrines teaching that there prevails, within the frame of the market economy, an irreconcilable conflict among the interests of any nation and those of all other nations. It is entirely wrong with regard to any kind of entrepreneurial profit or loss.

What produces a man's profit in the course of affairs within an unhampered market society is not his fellow citizen's plight and distress, but the fact that he alleviates or entirely removes what causes his fellow citizen's uneasiness. What hurts the sick is the plague, not the physician who treats the disease. The doctor's gain is not an outcome of the epidemics, but the aid he gives to those afflicted.

An excess of the total amount of profits over that of losses is a proof of the fact that there is economic progress and improvement in the standard of living of all strata of the population. The greater this excess is, the greater is the increment in general prosperity. Entrepreneurial profits and losses are essential phenomena of the market economy. There cannot be a market economy without them.

It is absurd to speak of a "rate of profit" or a "normal rate of profit." Profit is not related to or dependent on the amount of capital employed by the entrepreneur. Capital does not "beget" profit. Profit and loss are entirely determined by the success or failure of the entrepreneur to adjust production to the demand of the consumers. Entrepreneurial profits are not a lasting phenomenon but only temporary. There prevails an inherent tendency for profits and losses to disappear.

Profits Help the Economy

The entrepreneurial function, the striving of entrepreneurs after profits, is the driving power in the market economy. Profit and loss are the devices by means of which the consumers exercise their supremacy on the market. The behavior of the consumers makes profits and losses appear and thereby shifts ownership of the means of production from the hands of the less efficient into those of the more efficient.

Production for profit is necessarily production for use, as profits can only be earned by providing the consumers with those things they most urgently want to use....

On Socialism

Private ownership of the means of production (market economy or capitalism) and public ownership of the means of production (socialism or communism or "planning") can never be confounded with one another; they cannot be mixed or combined; no gradual transition leads from one of them to the other; they are mutually incompatible. With regard to the same factors of production there can only exist private control or public control.

In the first case there is a market, there are market prices for all factors of production, and economic calculation is possible. In the second case all these things are absent. It is vain to comfort oneself with the hope that the organs of the collective economy will be "omnipresent" and "omniscient." We do not deal in praxeology with the acts of the omnipresent and omniscient Deity, but with the actions of men endowed with a human mind only. Such a mind cannot plan without economic calculation.

A socialist system with a market and market prices is as self-contradictory as is the notion of a triangular square. The essential mark of socialism is that *one will* alone acts. It is immaterial whose will it is. The director may be an anointed king or a dictator, ruling by virtue of his *charisma*, he may be a Führer or a board of Führers appointed by the vote of the people. The main thing is that the employment of all factors of production is directed by one agency only. One will alone chooses, decides, directs, acts, gives orders and instruction. Organization and a planned order are substituted for the "anarchy" of production.

The Elimination of the Market

When the socialists declare that "order" and "organization" are to be substituted for the "anarchy" of production, conscious action for the alleged planlessness of capitalism, true cooperation for competition, production for use for production for profit, what they have in mind is the substitution of the exclusive and monopolistic power of only *one* agency for the infinite multitude of the plans of individual consumers and those attending to the wishes of the consumers, the entrepreneurs and capitalists. The essence of socialism is the entire elimination of the market and of catallactic competition. The socialist system is a system without a market or market prices for the factors of production, and without competition; it means the unrestricted centralization and unification of the conduct of all affairs in the hands of one authority....

The Best Way of Life

Democratic capitalism, combined with industrial democracy, is unquestionably the best way of life for mankind.

David J. McDonald, *New York Post*, October 20, 1957.

Private ownership of the means of production is the fundamental institution of the market economy. It is the institution which characterizes the market economy as such. Where it is absent, there is no question of a market economy.

In an economic system in which there is no private ownership of the means of production, no market, and no prices for goods, the concepts of capital and income are mere academic postulates devoid of any practical application. In a socialist economy there are capital goods but no capital.

The notion of capital makes sense only in the market economy. It serves the deliberations and calculations of individuals or groups of individuals operating on their own account in such an economy. It is a device of capitalists, entrepreneurs, and farmers eager to make profits and to avoid losses. Profit tells the entrepreneur that the consumers approve of his ventures; loss, that they disapprove.

The problem of socialist economic calculation is precisely this: that in the absence of market prices for the factors of production, a computation of profit or loss is not feasible. The paradox of "planning" is that it cannot plan, because of the absence of economic calculation. What is called a planned economy is no economy at all. It is just a system of groping in the dark.

Socialism cannot be realized because it is beyond human power to establish it as a social system. The choice is between capitalism and chaos. A man who chooses between drinking a glass of milk and a glass of potassium cyanide does not choose between two beverages; he chooses between life and death. A society that chooses between capitalism and socialism does not choose between two social systems; it can choose between social cooperation and the disintegration of society....

On Employment

The worker looks upon unemployment as an evil. He would like to avoid it provided the sacrifice is not too grievous. He chooses between employment and unemployment in the same way in which he proceeds in all other actions and choices: he weighs the pros and cons. If he chooses unemployment this unemployment is a market phenomenon whose nature is not different from other market phenomena as they appear in a changing market economy. We may call this kind of unemployment market-generated or *catallactic unemployment*.

Catallactic unemployment must not be confused with *institutional unemployment*. Institutional unemployment is not the outcome of the decisions of individual job-seekers. It is the effect of interference with the market phenomena intent upon enforcing by coercion and compulsion wage rates higher than those the unhampered market would have determined.

Higher Wages and Unemployment

Real wage rates can rise only to the extent that, other things being equal, capital becomes more plentiful. If the government or the unions succeed in enforcing wage rates which are higher than those the unhampered market would have determined, the supply of labor exceeds the demand for labor. Institutional unemployment emerges.

Firmly committed to the principles of interventionism, governments try to check this undesired result of their interference by resorting to those measures which are nowadays called full-employment policy: unemployment doles, arbitration of labor disputes, public works by means of lavish public spending, inflation and credit expansion. All these remedies are worse than the evil they are designed to remove.

Assistance granted to the unemployed does not dispose of unemployment. It makes it easier for the unemployed to remain idle. The nearer the allowance comes to the height at which the unhampered market would have fixed the wage rate, the less incentive it offers to the beneficiary to look for a new job. It is a means of making unemployment last rather than of making it disappear. The disastrous financial implications of unemployment benefits are manifest.

On the unhampered market there is always for each type of labor a rate at which all those eager to work can get a job. The final wage rate is that rate at which all jobs-seekers get jobs and all employers [get] as many workers as they want to hire. Its height is determined by the marginal productivity of each type of work.

Unemployment in the unhampered market is always voluntary....

On Wages

Wages are the price paid for the wage earner's achievement, i.e., for the contribution of his efforts to the processing of the good concerned or, as people say, for the value which his services add to the value of the materials. No matter whether there are time wages or piecework wages, the employer always buys the worker's performance and services, not his time.

Every employer must aim at buying the factors of production needed, inclusive of labor, at the cheapest price. An employer who paid more than agrees with the market price of the services his employees render him, would soon be removed from his entrepreneurial position. On the other hand an employer who tried to reduce wage rates below the heights consonant with the marginal productivity of labor would not recruit the type of man that the most efficient utilization of his equipment requires....

In the market economy the worker sells his services as other people sell their commodities. The employer is not the employee's lord. He is simply the buyer of services which he must purchase at their market price....

An employer cannot grant favors at the expense of his customers. He cannot pay wage rates higher than those determined by the market if the buyers are not ready to pay proportionately higher prices for commodities produced in plants in which wage rates are higher than in other plants.

"The market has always been one of exploitation and thereby of domination, insuring the class structure of society."

Capitalism Destroys Human Freedom

Herbert Marcuse

Herbert Marcuse was a professor of philosophy at the University of California at San Diego and a prominent political theorist. He was born in Berlin and educated at the Universities of Berlin and Freiburg. An avowed communist, Marcuse believed that capitalism, by its nature, was exploitative and oppressive. In the following viewpoint, excerpted from his book *An Essay on Liberation*, Marcuse argues that capitalism fosters a dependence on consumer goods. Because everyone in the society becomes accustomed to and in need of these goods, they have a vested interest in making sure capitalism continues. What is needed, argues Marcuse, is an entirely new way of thinking in which society moves from consumerism toward socialism. Only then will people enjoy real freedom and happiness.

As you read, consider the following questions:

1. Why does the author believe it is necessary to break with the established system in order for society to change?
2. How does capitalism dull man's incentive to change his environment, according to the author?

Utopian possibilities are inherent in the technical and technological forces of advanced capitalism and socialism: the rational utilization of these forces on a global scale would terminate poverty and scarcity within a very foreseeable future. But we know now that neither their rational use nor—and this is decisive—their collective control by the "immediate producers" (the workers) would by itself eliminate domination and exploitation: a bureaucratic welfare state would still be a state of repression which would continue even into the "second phase of socialism," when each is to receive "according to his needs."

What is now at stake are the needs themselves. At this stage, the question is no longer: how can the individual satisfy his own needs without hurting others, but rather: how can he satisfy his needs without hurting himself, without reproducing, through his aspirations and satisfactions, his dependence on an exploitative apparatus which, in satisfying his needs, perpetuates his servitude? The advent of a free society would be characterized by the fact that the growth of well-being turns into an essentially new quality of life....

We Can No Longer Tolerate This Society

Freedom would become the environment of an organism which is no longer capable of adapting to the competitive performances required for well-being under domination, no longer capable of tolerating the aggressiveness, brutality, and ugliness of the established way of life. The rebellion would then have taken root in the very nature, the "biology" of the individual; and on these new grounds, the rebels would redefine the objectives and the strategy of the political struggle, in which alone the concrete goals of liberation can be determined....

The world of human freedom cannot be built by the established societies, no matter how much they may streamline and rationalize their dominion. Their class structure, and the perfected controls required to sustain it, generate needs, satisfactions, and values which reproduce the servitude of the human existence. This "voluntary" servitude...which justifies the benevolent masters, can be broken only through a political practice which reaches the roots of containment and contentment in the infrastructure of man, a political practice of methodical disengagement from and refusal of the Establishment....Such a practice involves a break with the familiar, the routine ways of seeing, hearing, feeling, understanding things so that the organism may become receptive to the potential forms of a nonaggressive, nonexploitative world....

Capitalism Based on Exploitation

In the affluent society, capitalism comes into its own. The two mainsprings of its dynamic—the escalation of commodity production and productive exploitation—join and permeate all dimensions of private and public existence. The available material and intellectual resources (the potential of liberation) have so much outgrown the established institutions that only the systematic increase in waste, destruction, and management keeps the system going. The opposition which escapes suppression by the police, the courts, the representatives of the people, and the people themselves, finds expression in the diffused rebellion among the youth and the intelligentsia, and in the daily struggle of the persecuted minorities. The armed class struggle is waged outside: by the wretched of the earth who fight the affluent monster.

The critical analysis of this society calls for new categories: moral, political, aesthetic. I shall try to develop them in the course of the discussion. The category of obscenity will serve as an introduction.

Capitalism Is Obscene

This society is obscene in producing and indecently exposing a stifling abundance of wares while depriving its victims abroad of the necessities of life; obscene in stuffing itself and its garbage cans while poisoning and burning the scarce foodstuffs in the fields of its aggression; obscene in the words and smiles of its politicians and entertainers; in its prayers, in its ignorance, and in the wisdom of its kept intellectuals....

The Source of All Slavery

The subordination of labor to capital is the source of all slavery: political, moral and material.

Mikhail A. Bakunin.

The so-called consumer economy and the politics of corporate capitalism have created a second nature of man which ties him libidinally and aggressively to the commodity form. The need for possessing, consuming, handling, and constantly renewing the gadgets, devices, instruments, engines, offered to and imposed upon the people, for using these wares even at the danger of one's own destruction, has become a "biological" need in the sense just defined. The second nature of man thus militates against any change that would disrupt and perhaps even abolish this dependence of man on a market ever more densely filled with merchandise—abolish his existence as a consumer consuming himself in buying and selling. The needs generated by this system are thus eminently stabilizing, conservative needs: the counterrevolution anchored in the instinctual structure.

The market has always been one of exploitation and thereby of domination, insuring the class structure of society. However, the productive process of advanced capitalism has altered the form of domination: the technological veil covers the brute presence and

46

the operation of the class interest in the merchandise. Is it still necessary to state that not technology, not technique, not the machine are the engines of repression, but the presence, in them, of the masters who determine their number, their life span, their power, their place in life, and the need for them? Is it still necessary to repeat that science and technology are the great vehicles of liberation, and that it is only their use and restriction in the repressive society which makes them into vehicles of domination?

System, Not Products, Repressive

Not the automobile is repressive, not the television set is repressive, not the household gadgets are repressive, but the automobile, the television, the gadgets which, produced in accordance with the requirements of profitable exchange, have become part and parcel of the people's own existence, own "actualization." Thus they have to buy part and parcel of their own existence on the market; this existence is the realization of capital. The naked class interest builds the unsafe and obsolescent automobiles, and through them promotes destructive energy; the class interest employs the mass media for the advertising of violence and stupidity, for the creation of captive audiences. In doing so, the masters only obey the demand of the public, of the masses; the famous law of supply and demand establishes the harmony between the rulers and the ruled. This harmony is indeed preestablished to the degree to which the masters have created the public which asks for their wares, and asks for them more insistently if it can release, in and through the wares, its frustration and the aggressiveness resulting from this frustration. Self-determination, the autonomy of the individual, asserts itself in the right to race his automobile, to handle his power tools, to buy a gun, to communicate to mass audiences his opinion, no matter how ignorant, how aggressive, it may be. Organized capitalism has sublimated and turned to socially productive use frustration and primary aggressiveness on an unprecedented scale—unprecedented not in terms of the quantity of violence but rather in terms of its capacity to produce long-range contentment and satisfaction, to reproduce the "voluntary servitude." To be sure, frustration, unhappiness, and sickness remain the basis of this sublimation, but the productivity and the brute power of the system still keep the basis well under control. The achievements justify the system of domination. The established values become the people's own values: adaptation turns into spontaneity, autonomy; and the choice between social necessities appears as freedom. In this sense, the continuing exploitation is not only hidden behind the technological veil, but actually "transfigured." The capitalist production relations are responsible not only for the servitude and toil but also for the greater happiness and fun available to the majority of the population—and they deliver more goods than before.

Neither its vastly increased capacity to produce the commodities of satisfaction nor the peaceful management of class conflicts rendered possible by this capacity cancels the essential features of capitalism, namely, the private appropriation of surplus value (steered but not abolished by government intervention) and its realization in the corporate interest. Capitalism reproduces itself by transforming itself, and this transformation is mainly in the improvement of exploitation. Do exploitation and domination cease to be what they are and what they do to man if they are no longer suffered, if they are "compensated" by previously unknown comforts? Does labor cease to be debilitating if mental energy increasingly replaces physical energy in producing the goods and services which sustain a system that makes hell of large areas of the globe?...

Happiness...has been effectively obscured; its validity depends on the real solidarity of the species "man," which a society divided into antagonistic classes and nations cannot achieve....

Spanish Civil War as Example

The Spanish civil war aroused this solidarity, which is the driving power of liberation, in the unforgettable, hopeless fight of a tiny minority against the combined forces of fascist and liberal capitalism. Here, in the international brigades which, with their poor weapons, withstood overwhelming technical superiority, was the union of young intellectuals and workers—the union which has become the desperate goal of today's radical opposition.

Like a Vampire

Capital is dead labor, that vampire-like, only lives by sucking living labor.

Karl Marx, *Capital*, 1867.

Attainment of this goal is thwarted by the integration of the organized (and not only the organized) laboring class into the system of advanced capitalism. Under its impact, the distinction between the real and the immediate interest of the exploited has collapsed. This distinction, far from being an abstract idea, was guiding the strategy of the Marxist movements; it expressed the necessity transcending the economic struggle of the laboring classes, to extend wage demands and demands for the improvement of working conditions to the political arena, to drive the class struggle to the point at which the system itself would be at stake, to make foreign as well as domestic policy, the national as well as the class interest, the target of this struggle. The real interest, the attainment of conditions in which man could shape his own life, was that of no longer subordinating his life to the requirements of profitable production, to an apparatus controlled by forces beyond his control. And the attainment of such conditions meant the abolition of capitalism.

It is not simply the higher standard of living, the illusory bridging of the consumer gap between the rulers and the ruled, which has obscured the distinction between the real and the immediate interest of the ruled. Marxian theory soon recognized that impoverishment does not necessarily provide the soil for revolution, that a highly developed consciousness and imagination may generate a vital need for radical change in advanced material conditions. The power of corporate capitalism has stifled the emergence of such a consciousness and imagination; its mass media have adjusted the rational and emotional faculties to its market and its policies and steered them to defense of its dominion. The narrowing of the consumption gap has rendered possible the mental and instinctual coordination of the laboring classes: the majority of organized labor shares the stabilizing, counterrevolutionary needs of the middle classes, as evidenced by their behavior as consumers of the material and cultural merchandise, by their emotional revulsion against the nonconformist intelligentsia. Conversely, where the consumer gap is still wide, where the capitalist culture has not yet reached into every house or hut, the system of stabilizing needs has its limits; the glaring contrast between the privileged class and the exploited leads to a radicalization of the underprivileged. This is the case of the ghetto population and the unemployed in the United States; this is also the case of the laboring classes in the more backward capitalist countries....

A Vested Interest in the Existing System

In the advanced capitalist countries, the radicalization of the working classes is counteracted by a socially engineered arrest of consciousness, and by the development and satisfaction of needs which perpetuate the servitude of the exploited. A vested interest in the existing system is thus fostered in the instinctual structure of the exploited, and the rupture with the continuum of repression —a necessary precondition of liberation—does not occur. It follows that the radical change which is to transform the existing society into a free society must reach into a dimension of the human existence hardly considered in Marxian theory—the "biological" dimension in which the vital, imperative needs and satisfactions of man assert themselves. Inasmuch as these needs and satisfactions reproduce a life in servitude, liberation presupposes changes in this biological dimension, that is to say, different instinctual needs, different reactions of the body as well as the mind.

The qualitative difference between the existing societies and a free society affects all needs and satisfactions beyond the animal level, that is to say, all those which are essential to the *human* species, man as rational animal. All these needs and satisfactions are permeated with the exigencies of profit and exploitation. The entire realm of competitive performances and standardized fun, all the symbols of status, prestige, power, of advertised virility and charm, of commercialized beauty—this entire realm kills in its citizens the very disposition, the organs, for the alternative: freedom without exploitation....

Vicious Circle

Capitalist progress thus not only reduces the environment of freedom, the "open space" of the human existence, but also the "longing," the need for such an environment. And in doing so, quantitative progress militates against qualitative change even if the institutional barriers against radical education and action are surmounted. This is the vicious circle: the rupture with the self-propelling conservative continuum of needs must *precede* the revolution which is to usher in a free society, but such rupture itself can be envisaged only in a revolution—a revolution which would be driven by the vital need to be freed from the administered comforts and the destructive productivity of the exploitative society, freed from smooth heteronomy, a revolution which, by virtue of this "biological" foundation, would have the chance of turning quantitative technical progress into qualitatively different ways of life—precisely because it would be a revolution occurring at a high level of material and intellectual development, one which would enable man to conquer scarcity and poverty.

Evaluating Sources of Information

A critical thinker must always question sources of information. Historians, for example, usually distinguish between *primary sources (eyewitness accounts)* and *secondary sources (writings or statements based on primary or eyewitness accounts or on other secondary sources.)* A newly developed political theory, explained and published by its creator, is an example of a primary source. A newspaper article describing that theory is a secondary source.

In order to read and think critically, one must be able to recognize primary sources. However, this is not enough. Eyewitness accounts do not always provide accurate descriptions. Historians may find ten different eyewitness accounts of an event and all the accounts might interpret the event differently. The historians must then decide which of these accounts provide the most objective and accurate interpretations.

Test your skills in evaluating sources of information by completing the following exercise. Pretend that your teacher assigns you to write a research report comparing capitalism and communism. You decide to include an equal number of primary and secondary sources. Listed below are a number of sources which may be useful in your research. Carefully evaluate each of them. *Then, place a P next to those descriptions you believe are primary sources. Second, rank the primary sources assigning the number (1) to what appears to be the most objective and accurate primary source, the number (2) to the next most objective, and so on until the ranking is finished. Repeat the entire procedure, this time placing an S next to those descriptions you feel would serve as secondary sources and then ranking them.*

If you are doing this activity as a member of a class or group, discuss and compare your evaluation with other members of the group. If you are reading this book alone, you may want to ask others if they agree with your evaluation. You will probably discover that others will come to different conclusions than you. Listening to their reasons may give you valuable insights in evaluating sources of information.

$$P = primary$$
$$S = secondary$$

1. an 1844 pamphlet titled "The Manifesto of the Communist Party"

2. a book called *The History of the Communist Movement*

3. a reprint of a lecture to a group of college political science professors on "In Praise of Capitalism"

4. testimony given by a wealthy manufacturer before a Congressional committee defending the buildup of monopolies

5. an autobiographical work written by a woman who was a journalist and lived in both the United States and the USSR

6. the Constitution of the United States

7. an eyewitness account smuggled out of Poland to a US newspaper describing living conditions in Poland right after the Socialist takeover

8. a biography of Karl Marx

9. viewpoint 1 from this chapter

10. a movie produced by Steven Spielberg on the Communist Revolution in 1917 Russia

11. a documentary film on union labor in Britain

12. a newspaper article written by Richard Nixon that explains American intervention in Vietnam

13. a television interview with actress Shirley Maclaine after her first visit to Communist China

14. a corporate report detailing the company's branch plants in South Africa

15. a *Time* magazine article presenting an overview of Soviet-American relations over the past fifty years

16. a research paper written for this class last year by your sister

17. a book called *The Impact of Communism on Cuba*

18. a chart showing statistics on the average educations, including incomes, and lifespans of people in eighty different countries, some communist and some capitalist

Bibliography

The following bibliography deals with the subject matter of this chapter.

John Elster	*Making Sense of Marx*. New York: Cambridge University Press, 1985.
Eric Hobsbawn	*History of Marxism: Marxism in Marx's Day*. Bloomington, IN: Indiania University Press, 1982.
Irving Howe	*Socialism and America*. New York: Harcourt, Brace, Jovanovich, 1985.
Arthur Jenkins	*Adam Smith Today: An Inquiry into the Nature and Causes of the Wealth of Nations*. New York: R.R. Smith, 1948.
J. Ralph Lindgren	*The Early Writings of Adam Smith*. New York: A.M. Kelley, 1967.
Steven Lukes	*Marxism and Morality*. New York: Clarendon Press, 1985.
Herbert Marcuse	*One Dimensional Man: Studies in the Ideology of Advanced Industrial Society*. Boston: Beacon Press, 1964.
Karl Marx	*On Society and Social Change*. Chicago: University of Chicago Press, 1973.
Ayn Rand	*The Virtue of Selfishness*. New York: Signet Books, 1961.
Ayn Rand	*Atlas Shrugged*. New York: Random House, 1957.
D.D. Raphael	*Adam Smith*. New York: Oxford University Press, 1985.
Jon Roemer, ed.	*Analytical Marxism*. New York: Cambridge University Press, 1985.
Hubert Schneider	*Adams Smith's Moral and Political Philosophy*. New York: Hafner Publishing Co., 1948.
Adam Smith	*Essays: Philosophical and Literary*. London: Ward, Lock and Co.
Robert Paul Wolff	*Understanding Marx: A Reconstruction and Critique of 'Capital.'* Princeton, NJ: Princeton University Press, 1985.

Capitalism and Labor in the Nineteenth Century

Introduction

The Industrial Revolution and the accompanying rise of capitalism brought about profound changes in the economic and social order of Western European society. Experiencing little or no governmental interference, the early industries flourished and, as prophesied by Adam Smith, so did the wealth of nations. The success of the new system resulted from the efforts of two highly distinguishable classes, the capitalists who financed the industries and the workers who were employed within them. In the nineteenth century, however, the capitalists, for the most part, were the system's prime beneficiaries. The nature of early industry was such that the profits enjoyed by the owners were generated by the toil of the hapless workers. (There were notable exceptions, however. Foremost among them was Robert Owen, a British industrialist who rose from a laborer in a cotton factory to part-owner of a mill in New Lanark, Scotland. Mindful of his humble origin, Owen took an active interest in the welfare of his workers and converted New Lanark into a model factory town.)

In the absence of governmental regulation and effective employee organizations, working conditions were usually extremely poor and wages dismally low. The work day averaged twelve to fourteen hours and ran as high as nineteen hours during busy periods. Women and children were employed under conditions similar to men, receiving only half to a quarter of the wages paid men. In most factories, the machinery was propelled by large gear wheels which often had no protective coverings. It was not unusual for a worker to mangle or lose a finger, hand or arm in one of these machines. There were no benefits such as sick leave and worker's compensation. Indeed, an individual injured on the job was required to meet his or her own medical expenses and suffer a complete salary loss while recuperating. Finally, the living

Before the days of child labor laws, women and children work in a bean processing plant (c. 1900).

United Press International, Inc.

conditions of the worker were as impoverished as the working conditions.

The following viewpoints attempt to illustrate the socio-economic circumstances of nineteenth-century labor. The viewpoints supportive of capitalism defend the system on the basis of natural law, the merits of "self-help," and the visible improvement it represented over the previous period. The opposing viewpoints look no further than the worker to underscore their assertion that radical reform was morally imperative.

"Since the comfortable wages of factory labor have begun to be enjoyed, the mortality has diminished...that is, only three persons die now, where four died in the golden age of precarious rural or domestic employment."

England Is a Worker's Paradise

Andrew Ure

Andrew Ure was one of England's staunchest defenders of the factory system. Born in Scotland, he received his M.D. from Edinburgh University in 1801 and went on to teach chemistry and natural philosophy at Anderson's College, in Glasgow. Ure wrote and lectured extensively on popular scientific subjects in an effort to enlighten the common person of his day. In the following viewpoint, excerpted from his *Philosophy of Manufactures*, he takes the position that the living and working standards in nineteenth-century England were far better than those of the pre-industrial age.

As you read, consider the following questions:

1. What does the author believe are the blessings of the machine age?
2. How, according to the author, are children treated in the factories?
3. Does the author believe that wages are good in the factories? Why or why not?

Andrew Ure, *The Philosophy of Manufacturers*, London: Frank Cass & Co., 1967. Reprinted with permission.

This island [England] is pre-eminent among civilized nations for the prodigious development of its factory wealth, and has been therefore long viewed with a jealous admiration by foreign powers. This very pre-eminence, however, has been contemplated in a very different light by many influential members of our own community, and has been even denounced by them as the certain origin of innumerable evils to the people, and of revolutionary convulsions to the state. If the affairs of the kingdom be wisely administered, I believe such allegations and fears will prove to be groundless, and to proceed more from the envy of one ancient and powerful order of the commonwealth [aristocracy], towards another suddenly grown into political importance than from the nature of things [bourgeoisie]....

The blessings which physico-mechanical science has bestowed on society, and the means it has still in store for ameliorating the lot of mankind, have been too little dwelt upon; while, on the other hand, it has been accused of lending itself to the rich capitalists as an instrument for harassing the poor, and of exacting from the operative an accelerated rate of work. It has been said, for example, that the steam-engine now drives the power-looms with such velocity as to urge on their attendant weavers at the same rapid pace; but that the hand-weaver, not being subjected to this restless agent, can throw his shuttle and move his treddles at his convenience. There is, however, this difference in the two cases; that in the factory, every member of the loom is so adjusted that the driving force leaves the attendant nearly nothing at all to do, certainly no muscular fatigue to sustain, while it procures for him good, un-failing wages, besides a healthy workshop *gratis:* whereas the non-factory weaver, having everything to execute by muscular exertion, finds the labor irksome, makes in consequence innumerable short pauses, separately of little account, but great when added together; earns therefore proportionally low wages, while he loses his health by poor diet and the dampness of his hovel. Dr. Carbutt of Man-chester says, "With regard to Sir Robert Peel's assertion a few even-ings ago, that the handloom weavers are mostly small farmers, nothing can be a greater mistake; they live, or rather they just keep life together, in the most miserable manner, in the cellars and gar-rets of the town, working sixteen or eighteen hours for the merest pittance."...

Kindness Toward Children

Nothing shows in a clearer point of view the credulity of man-kind in general, and of the people of these islands in particular, than the ready faith which was given to the tales of cruelty exercised by proprietors of cotton-mills towards young children....The mill-owner, in fact, could never interfere but beneficially for the children....

I have visited many factories, both in Manchester and in the surrounding districts, during a period of several months, entering the spinning rooms unexpectedly, and often alone, at different times of the day, and I never saw a single instance of corporal chastisement inflicted on a child, nor indeed did I ever see children in ill-humor. They seemed to be always cheerful and alert, taking pleasure in the light play of their muscles—enjoying the mobility natural to their age. The scene of industry, so far from exciting sad emotions in my mind, was always exhilarating. It was delightful to observe the nimbleness with which they pieced the broken ends, as the mule-carriage began to recede from the fixed roller-beam,

---

Scientific Improvement

The constant aim and effect of scientific improvement in manufactures are philanthropic, as they tend to relieve the workmen either from niceties of adjustment which exhaust his mind and fatigue his eyes, or from painful repetition of effort which distort or wear out his frame.

Andrew Ure.

---

and to see them at leisure, after a few seconds' exercise of their tiny fingers, to amuse themselves in any attitude they chose, till the stretch and winding-on were once more completed. The work of these lively elves seemed to resemble a sport, in which habit gave them a pleasing dexterity. Conscious of their skill, they were delighted to show it off to any stranger. As to exhaustion by the day's work, they evinced no trace of it on emerging from the mill in the evening; for they immediately began to skip about any neighboring playground, and to commence their little amusements with the same alacrity as boys issuing from a school. It is moreover my firm conviction that if children are not ill-used by bad parents or guardians, but receive in food and raiment the full benefit of what they earn, they would thrive better when employed in our modern factories than if left at home in apartments too often ill aired, damp, and cold....

A Low Death Rate

The mortality of that town [Leeds, an industrial town in northern England] has diminished since 1801, at which time there were scarcely any manufactories established in it. The population of the township was in 1801, 30,669; and the burials of the three years preceding being 2882, or 941 annually, the resulting rate of mortality is one in thirty-two and a half. In 1831 the population was 71,602, and the burials of the three years preceding were 5153, or 1718 annually, giving a rate of mortality of one in forty-one and a half. Thus, since the comfortable wages of factory labor have begun to be enjoyed, the mortality has diminished in the proportion of thirty-two and a half to forty-one and a half; that is, only three persons die now, where four died in the golden age of precarious rural or domestic employment....

Good Food and Sanitation

It seems established by a body of incontestable evidence that the wages of our factory work-people, if prudently spent, would enable them to live in a comfortable manner, and decidedly better than formerly, in consequence of the relative diminution in the price of food, fuel, lodgings, and clothing....

And as to the charge which has been made of the injury done to their constitutions by entering a factory in early life, the following refutation of it is most decisive. "There is one thing I feel convinced of from observation, that young persons, especially females, who have begun mill-work at from ten to twelve, independently of their becoming much more expert artists, preserve their health better, and possess sounder feet and legs at twenty-five than those who have commenced from thirteen to sixteen and upwards."

"At the Blantyre mills," says the same competent observer, "the spinners are all males. I visited the dwellings of nine of that class without making any selection. Found that every one of them was married, and that the wife had been in every instance a mill-girl, some of these women having begun factory work as early as at six and a half years of age. The number of children born to these nine couples was fifty one; the number now living forty-six. As many of these children as are able to work, and can find vacancies, are employed in the mill. They all live in rooms rented from the owners, and are well lodged. I saw them at breakfast time, and the meal was composed of the following: viz., porridge and milk for the children; coffee, eggs, bread, oaten cake, and butter for the father."

2

"More than fifty-seven per cent of the children of the working class and not quite thirty-two per cent of the children of all classes in the country die under five years of age."

England Is a Worker's Hell

Friedrich Engels

A German-born economist and socialist, Friedrich Engels, along with Karl Marx, was the dominant figure in the nineteenth-century communist movement. Engels was converted to communism at the age of twenty-one by Moses Hess, a leading German intellectual. Engels moved to England, where he identified himself with trade unions and radical reform movements. An industrialist in his early years, he withdrew from business in 1844 and began a lifelong association with Marx. Upon Marx's death, he completed, edited, and published many of Marx's works, including volumes II and III of *Das Kapital*. In the following viewpoint, Engels offers an account of the depressed condition of England's working classes.

As you read, consider the following questions:

1. What was England like before the machine age, according to the author?
2. How does the author describe working conditions after the machine age?
3. What does the author quote the Central Commission as saying about living conditions?

Friedrich Engels, *The Conditions of the Working Class*, Hemel Hempstead: England: George Allen & Unwin Ltd., 1925. Reprinted with permission.

The history of the proletariat in England begins with the second half of the last century [eighteenth century], with the invention of the steam-engine and of machinery for working cotton. These inventions gave rise, as is well known, to an industrial revolution, a revolution which altered the whole civil society; one, the historical importance of which is only now beginning to be recognised. England is the classic soil of this transformation, which was all the mightier, the more silently it proceeded; and England is, therefore, the classic land of its chief product also, the proletariat. Only in England can the proletariat be studied in all its relations and from all sides....

Before the introduction of machinery, the spinning and weaving of raw materials was carried on in the workingman's home. Wife and daughter spun the yarn that the father wove or that they sold, if he did not work it up himself. These weaver families lived in the country in the neighborhood of the towns, and could get on fairly well with their wages....So it was that the weaver was usually in a position to lay by something and rent a little piece of land that he cultivated in his leisure hours, of which he had as many as he chose to take, since he could weave whenever and as long as he pleased. True, he was a bad farmer and managed his land inefficiently, often obtaining but poor crops; nevertheless, he was no proletarian, he had a stake in the country, he was permanently settled, and stood one step higher in society than the English workman of today.

So the workers vegetated throughout a passably comfortable existence, leading a righteous and peaceful life in all piety and probity; and their material position was far better than that of their successors. They did not need to overwork; they did no more than they chose to do, and yet earned what they needed. They had leisure for healthful work in garden or field, work which, in itself, was recreation for them, and they could take part besides in the recreations and games of their neighbors, and all these games, bowling, cricket, football, etc., contributed to their physical health and vigor. They were, for the most part, strong, well-built people, in whose physique little or no difference from that of their peasant neighbors was discoverable. Their children grew up in the fresh country air and, if they could help their parents at work, it was only occasionally; while of eight or twelve hours work for them there was no question....

Cruelty Toward Children

The report of the Central Commission relates that the manufacturers began to employ children rarely of five years, often of six, very often of seven, usually of eight to nine years; that the working-day often lasted fourteen to sixteen hours, exclusive of meals and intervals; that the manufacturers permitted overlookers to flog and maltreat children, and often took an active part in so doing themselves. One case is related of a Scotch manufacturer who rode after

F. Engels

a sixteen years old runaway, forced him to return running before the employer as fast as the master's horse trotted, and beat him the whole way with a long whip....

Every great city has one or more slums where the working class is crowded together. True, poverty often dwells in hidden alleys close to the palaces of the rich; but, in general, a separate territory has been assigned to it, where, removed from the sight of the happier classes, it may struggle along as it can. These slums are pretty equally arranged in all the great towns of England, the worst houses in the worst quarters of the towns; usually one or two-storied cottages in long rows, perhaps with cellars used as dwellings, almost always irregularly built. These houses of three or four rooms and a kitchen form, throughout England, some parts of London excepted, the general dwellings of the working class. The streets are generally unpaved, rough, dirty, filled with vegetable and animal refuse, without sewers or gutters, but supplied with foul stagnant pools instead. Moreover, ventilation is impeded by the bad, confused method of building of the whole quarter, and since many human beings here lived crowded into a small space, the atmosphere that prevails in these working-men's quarters may readily be imagined....

The death rate is kept so high chiefly by the heavy mortality among young children in the working class. The tender frame of a child is least able to withstand the unfavorable influences of an inferior lot in life; the neglect to which they are often subjected, when both parents work or one is dead, avenges itself promptly, and no one need wonder that in Manchester, according to the report last quoted, more than fifty-seven per cent of the children of the working class and not quite thirty-two per cent of the children of all classes in the country die under five years of age....

Poor Food and Sanitation

When one remembers under what conditions the working people live, when one thinks how crowded their dwellings are, how every nook and corner swarms with human beings, how sick and well sleep in the same room, in the same bed, the only wonder is that a contagious disease like...fever does not spread yet further....

Another category of diseases arises directly from the food rather than the dwellings of the workers. The food of the laborer, indigestible enough in itself, is utterly unfit for young children, and he has neither means nor time to get his children more suitable food.... Scrofula is almost universal among the working class, and scrofulous parents have scrofulous children, especially when the original influences continue in full force to operate upon the inherited tendency of the children. How greatly all these evils are increased by the chances to which the workers are subject in consequence of fluctuations in trade, want of work, and the scanty wages of times of crisis, it is not necessary to dwell upon. Temporary want of sufficient food, to which almost every workingman is exposed at least once in the course of his life, only contributes to intensify the effects of his usual sufficient but bad diet. Children who are half starved just when they most need ample and nutritious food—and how many such there are during every crisis and even when trade is at its best—must inevitably become weak, scrofulous, and rachitic in a high degree. And that they do become so, their appearance amply shows. The neglect to which the great mass of workingmen's children are condemned leaves ineradicable traces and brings the enfeeblement of the whole race of workers with it. Add to this the unsuitable clothing of this class, the impossibility of precautions against colds, the necessity of toiling so long as health permits, want made more dire when sickness appears and the only too common lack of medical assistance; and we have a rough idea of the sanitary condition of the English working class.

"National progress is the sum of individual industry, energy and uprightness, as national decay is of individual idleness, selfishness, and vice."

The Merit of Self-Help

Samuel Smiles

A popular philosophy in the Victorian era centered on that of individual self-help. Many Victorians believed all any person needed to achieve financial and social success was, not money or influence, but sheer individual effort. In the following viewpoint, Samuel Smiles, a Scottish biographer and essayist, articulates the popular theory of his day which holds that through perserverance and courage anyone could achieve success.

As you read, consider the following questions:

1. What does the author believe the role of government should be?
2. What are the great social evils, according to the author?

Samuel Smiles, *Self-Help, With Illustrations of Character*, New York: Harper & Row, 1874.

"Heaven helps those who help themselves" is a well-tried maxim, embodying in a small compass the results of vast human experience. The spirit of self-help is the root of all genuine growth in the individual; and, exhibited in the lives of many, it constitutes the true source of national vigor and strength. Help from without is often enfeebling in its effects, but help from within invariably invigorates. Whatever is done *for* men or classes, to a certain extent takes away the stimulus and necessity of doing for themselves; and where men are subjected to overguidance and over-government, the inevitable tendency is to render them comparatively helpless.

Even the best institutions can give a man no active help. Perhaps the most they can do is, to leave him free to develop himself and improve his individual condition. But in all times men have been prone to believe that their happiness and well-being were to be secured by means of institutions rather than by their own conduct. Hence the value of legislation as an agent in human advancement has usually been much over-estimated. To constitute the millionth part of a Legislature, by voting for one or two men once in three or five years, however conscientiously this duty may be performed, can exercise but little active influence upon any man's life and character. Moreover, it is every day becoming more clearly understood, that the function of Government is negative and restrictive, rather than positive and active; being resolvable principally into protection—protection of life, liberty, and property. Laws, wisely administered, will secure men in the enjoyment of the fruits of their labor, whether of mind or body, at a comparatively small personal sacrifice; but no laws, however stringent, can make the idle industrious, the thriftless provident, or the drunken sober. Such reforms can only be effected by means of individual action, economy, and self-denial; by better habits, rather than by greater rights.

No Government Interference

The Government of a nation itself is usually found to be but the reflex of the individuals composing it. The Government that is ahead of the people will inevitably be dragged down to their level, as the Government that is behind them will in the long run be dragged up. In the order of nature, the collective character of a nation will as surely find its befitting results in its law and government, as water finds its own level. The noble people will be nobly ruled, and the ignorant and corrupt ignobly. Indeed, all experience serves to prove that the worth and strength of a State depend far less upon the form of its institutions than upon the character of its men. For the nation is only an aggregate of individual conditions, and civilization itself is but a question of the personal improvement of the men, women, and children of whom society is composed.

National progress is the sum of individual industry, energy, and uprightness, as national decay is of individual idleness, selfishness, and vice. What we are accustomed to decry as great social evils, will for the most part be found to be but the outgrowth of man's own perverted life; and though we may endeavor to cut them down and extirpate them by means of Law, they will only spring up again with fresh luxuriance in some other form, unless the conditions of personal life and character are radically improved. If this view be correct, then it follows that the highest patriotism and philanthropy consists, not so much in altering laws and modifying institutions, as in helping and stimulating men to elevate and improve themselves by their own free and independent individual action.

All Work Is Noble

All work, even cotton-spinning, is noble; work is alone noble.

Thomas Carlyle, *Past and Present.*

It may be of comparatively little consequence how a man is governed from without, whilst every thing depends upon how he governs himself from within. The greatest slave is not he who is ruled by a despot, great though that evil be, but he who is the thrall of his own moral ignorance, selfishness, and vice. Nations who are thus enslaved at heart can not be freed by any mere changes of masters or of institutions....The solid Foundation of liberty must rest upon individual character; which is also the only sure guaranty for social security and national progress. John Stuart Mill truly observes that "even despotism does not produce its worst effects so long as individuality exists under it; and whatever crushes individuality is despotism, by whatever name it be called."

"The dread of being beaten if we could not keep up with our work was a sufficient impulse to keep us to it if we could."

The Need for Governmental Help

The Sadler Committee

The deplorable working conditions in England's mines and factories early in the nineteenth century prompted a series of parliamentary investigations. Several committees were formed to inquire into the gravity of the situation, especially where it concerned women and children. The findings of these committees created a scandal which shocked Parliament into enacting factory legislation aimed at correcting the abuses. The following testimony of two workers was presented in evidence before the Sadler Committee in 1832.

As you read, consider the following questions:

1. After reading this viewpoint and the previous viewpoint, do you think that governmental intervention was needed to help the nineteenth-century factory workers?
2. Do you believe certain jobs today keep people poor and downtrodden? Which jobs? Would governmental interference help these people?

Raymond Phineas, *Pageant of Europe*, New York: Harcourt, Brace & World, Inc., 1961. Reprinted with permission.

Mr. Matthew Crabtree, called in; and examined:

What age are you? — Twenty-two.

What is your occupation? — A blanket manufacturer.

Have you ever been employed in a factory? — Yes.

At what age did you first go to work in one? — Eight.

How long did you continue in that occupation? — Four years.

Will you state the hours of labour at the period when you first went to the factory, in ordinary times? — From 6 in the morning to 8 at night.

Fourteen hours? — Yes.

With what intervals for refreshment and rest? — An hour at noon.

When trade was brisk what were your hours? — From 5 in the morning to 9 in the evening.

Sixteen hours? — Yes....

How far did you live from the mill? — About two miles.

Was there any time allowed for you to get your breakfast in the mill? — No.

Did you take it before you left your home? — Generally.

During those long hours of labour could you be punctual; how did you awake? — I seldom did awake spontaneously; I was most generally awoke or lifted out of bed, sometimes asleep, by my parents.

Were you always in time? — No.

What was the consequence if you had been too late? — I was most commonly beaten.

Severely? — Very severely, I thought.

In those mills is chastisement towards the latter part of the day going on perpetually? — Perpetually.

So that you can hardly be in a mill without hearing constant crying? — Never an hour, I believe.

Beatings Are Necessary

Do you think that if the overlooker were naturally a humane person it would be still found necessary for him to beat the children, in order to keep up their attention and vigilance at the termination of those extraordinary days of labour? — Yes; the machine turns off a regular quantity of cardings, and of course they must keep as regularly to their work the whole of the day; they must keep with the machine, and therefore however humane the slubber may be, as he must keep up with the machine or be found fault with, he spurs the children to keep up also by various means but that which he commonly resorts to is to strap them when they become drowsy.

At the time when you were beaten for not keeping up with your work, were you anxious to have done it if you possibly could? — Yes; the dread of being beaten if we could not keep up with our work was a sufficient impulse to keep us to it if we could.

When you got home at night after this labour, did you feel much fatigued? — Very much so.

Had you any time to be with your parents, and to receive instruction from them? — No.

What did you do? — All that we did when we got home was to get the little bit of supper that was provided for us and go to bed immediately. If the supper had not been ready directly, we should have gone to sleep while it was preparing.

Did you not, as a child, feel it a very grievous hardship to be roused so soon in the morning? — I did.

At one time children formed one third of the industrial labor force in America. Young boys working at midnight in an Indiana glassworks factory, 1908.

Wide World Photos

Were the rest of the children similarly circumstanced? — Yes, all of them; but they were not all of them so far from their work as I was.

And if you had been too late you were under the apprehension of being cruelly beaten? — I generally was beaten, when I happened to be too late; and when I got up in the morning the apprehension of that was so great, that I used to run, and cry all the way as I went to the mill.

The Evidence of Samuel Coulson

At what time in the morning, in the brisk time, did those girls go to the mills? — In the brisk time, for about six weeks, they have gone at 3 o'clock in the morning, and ended at 10, or nearly half-past, at night.

What intervals were allowed for rest or refreshment during those nine-teen hours of labour? — Breakfast a quarter of an hour, and dinner half an hour, and drinking a quarter of an hour....

Had you not great difficulty in awakening your children to this ex-cessive labour? — Yes, in the early time we had them to take up asleep and shake them, when we got them on the floor to dress them, before we could get them off to their work; but not so in the common hours.

Supposing they had been a little too late, what would have been the consequence during the long hours? — They were quartered in the longest hours the same as in the shortest time.

What do you mean by quartering? — A quarter taken off.

If they had been how much too late? — Five minutes.

What was the length of time they could be in bed during those long hours? — It was near 11 o'clock before we could get them into bed after getting a little victuals, and then at morning my mistress used to stop up all night, for fear we could not get them ready for the time; sometimes we have gone to bed, and one of us generally awoke.

What time did you get them up in the morning? — In general me or my mistress got up at 2 o'clock to dress them.

So that they had not above four hours sleep at this time? — No, they had not.

A State of Slavery

Let the truth speak out, appalling as the statements may appear. Thousands of our fellow-creatures and fellow-subjects...are at this very moment existing in a state of slavery more horrid than are the victims of that hellish system, colonial slavery....Thousands of little children...are daily compelled to labour from 6 o'clock in the morn-ing to 7 o'clock in the evening with only—British, blush while you read it—with only 30 minutes allowed for eating and recreation.

Richard Oastler, *Slavery in Yorkshire.*

For how long together was it? — About six weeks it held; it was done only when the throng was very much on; it was not often that.

The common hours of labour were from 6 in the morning till half-past eight at night? — Yes.

With the same intervals for food? — Yes, just the same.

Were the children excessively fatigued by this labour? — Many times; we have cried often when we have given them the little victual-ling we had to give them; we had to shake them, and they have fallen asleep with the victuals in their mouths many a time.

Had any of them any accident in consequence of this labour? — Yes, my eldest daughter...the cog caught her forefinger nail and screwed it off below the knuckle, and she was five weeks in the Leeds infirmary.

Has she lost that finger? — It is cut off at the second joint.

Were her wages paid during that time? — As soon as the accident happened the wages were totally stopped; indeed, I did not know which way to get her cured....

Did this excessive term of labour occasion much cruelty also? — Yes, with being so much fatigued the strap was very frequently used.

Have any of your children been strapped? — Yes, every one; the eldest daughter; I was up in Lancashire a fortnight, and when I got home I saw her shoulders, and I said, "Ann, what is the matter?" She said, "the overlooker has strapped me; but," she said, "do not go to the overlooker, for if you do we shall lose our work."...Her back was beat nearly to a jelly....

What was the wages in the short hours? — Three shillings a week each.

When they wrought those very long hours what did they get? — Three shillings and sevenpence halfpenny.

For all that additional labour they had only 7½ pence a week additional? — No more.

"We accept and welcome...great inequality of environment, the concentration of business ...in the hands of a few...as being...essential for the future progress of the race."

Inequality Between Rich and Poor Is Natural

Andrew Carnegie

Andrew Carnegie presents one of the most extraordinary success stories in American history. A Scottish immigrant, he was a laborer in a cotton factory, a messenger for a telegraph company, and a railroad worker before eventually becoming the leading iron and steel manufacturer in the United States. Carnegie was a shrewd businessman who possessed a boundless and unwavering faith in America as a land of opportunity. His success as an industrialist was equaled by his generosity as a philanthropist. Convinced that the wealthy had a responsibility to society, Carnegie was directly responsible for the creation of philanthropic foundations worth in excess of one billion dollars. In the following viewpoint, Mr. Carnegie argues that the great disparity of wealth among people is a natural state, and not, as some people argued, imposed upon humanity by selfish capitalists.

As you read, consider the following questions:

1. What revolutionary changes does the author believe have taken place?
2. What does the author believe to be the price society must pay for these changes and why should society accept this price?

Andrew Carnegie, "Wealth," *North American Review*, June 1889.

The conditions of human life have not only been changed, but revolutionized, within the past few hundred years. In former days there was little difference between the dwelling, dress, food, and environment of the chief and those of his retainers....The contrast between the palace of the millionaire and the cottage of the laborer with us to-day measures the change which has come with civilization.

The change, however, is not to be deplored, but welcomed as highly beneficial. It is well, nay, essential for the progress of the race, that the houses of some should be homes for all that is highest and best in literature and the arts, and for all the refinements of civilization, rather than that none should be so. Much better this great irregularity than universal squalor....But whether the change be for good or ill, it is upon us, beyond our power to alter, and therefore to be accepted and made the best of. It is a waste of time to criticise the inevitable....

The Price of Change

The price we pay for this salutary change is, no doubt, great. We assemble thousands of operatives in the factory, in the mine, and in the counting-house, of whom the employer is little better than a myth. All intercourse between them is at an end. Rigid Castes are formed, and, as usual, mutual ignorance breeds mutual distrust. Each Caste is without sympathy for the other, and ready to credit anything disparaging in regard to it. Under the law of competition, the employer of thousands is forced into the strictest economies, among which the rates paid to labor figures prominently, and often there is friction between the employer and the employed, between capital and labor, between rich and poor. Human society loses homogeneity.

The price which society pays for the law of competition, like the price it pays for cheap comforts and luxuries, is also great; but the advantages of this law are also greater still, for it is to this law that we owe our wonderful material development, which brings improved conditions in its train. But, whether the law be benign or not, we must say of it, as we say of the change in the conditions of men to which we have referred: It is here; we cannot evade it; no substitutes for it have been found; and while the law may be sometimes hard for the individual, it is best for the race, because it insures the survival of the fittest in every department. We accept and welcome, therefore, as conditions to which we must accommodate ourselves, great inequality of environment, the concentration of business, industrial and commercial, in the hands of a few, and the law of competition between these, as being not only beneficial, but essential for the future progress of the race....

Objections to the foundations upon which society is based are not in order, because the condition of the race is better with these than it has been with any others which have been tried. Of the effect of any new substitutes proposed we cannot be sure. The Socialist or Anarchist who seeks to overturn present conditions is to be regarded as attacking the foundation upon which civilization itself rests, for civilization took its start from the day that the capable, industrious workman said to his incompetent and lazy fellow, "If thou dost not sow, thou shalt not reap," and thus ended primitive Communism by separating the drones from the bees....Good has come to the race from the accumulation of wealth by those who have the ability and energy that produce it. But even if we admit for a moment that it might be better for the race to discard its present foundation, Individualism,—that it is a nobler ideal that man should labor, not for himself alone, but in and for a brotherhood of his fellows, and share with them all in common, realizing Swedenborg's idea of Heaven, where, as he said, the angels derive

Andrew Carnegie rose from poverty to become a steel tycoon and philanthropist.

their happiness, not from laboring for self, but for each other,—even admit all this, and a sufficient answer is, This is not evolution, but revolution. It necessitates the changing of human nature itself—a work of aeons, even if it were good to change it, which we cannot know. It is not practicable in our day or in our age. Even if desirable theoretically, it belongs to another and long-succeeding sociological stratum. Our duty is with what is practicable now; with the next step possible in our day and generation. It is criminal to waste our energies in endeavoring to uproot, when all we can profitably or possibly accomplish is to bend the universal tree of humanity a little in the direction most favorable to the production of good fruit under existing circumstances. We might as well urge the destruction of the highest existing type of man because he failed to reach our ideal as to favor the destruction of Individualism, Private Property, the Law of Accumulation of Wealth, and the Law of Competition; for these are the highest result of human experience, the soil in which society so far has produced the best fruit. Unequally or unjustly, perhaps, as these laws sometimes operate, and imperfect as they appear to the Idealist, they are, nevertheless, like the highest type of man the best and most valuable of all that humanity has yet accomplished.

"In suffocating cellars...you might see men and women and children bending over whirling machines...breathing their lungs full of the fine dust, and doomed to die."

Inequality Is Imposed Through Capitalist Exploitation

Upton Sinclair

Upton Sinclair was an American author who actively crusaded against the social and economic ills in the US. Born in Baltimore, MD of a prominent but improverished family, he supported himself while in college by writing dime novels. Sinclair devoted his adult life to the cause of socialism and, in 1934, was nearly elected governor of California on his socialistic platform. His most famous work, *The Jungle*, is an exposé of conditions in the Chicago meat-packing industry at the turn of the century. The book was an attempt to illustrate the need for enforced humane working conditions and fair wages. The following excerpt from the book describes the plight of Jurgis, a Lithuanian immigrant, during his first days of work at the infamous fertilizer plant.

As you read, consider the following questions:

1. How is the fertilizer plant described?
2. Do you believe that Jurgis had a choice about working in the plant? Why or why not?

Upton Sinclair, *The Jungle*, New York: New American Library, 1905. By permission of Bertha Klausner International Literary Agency, Inc.

All this while that he was seeking for work, there was a dark shadow hanging over Jurgis; as if a savage beast were lurking somewhere in the pathway of his life, and he knew it, and yet could not help approaching the place. There are all stages of being out of work in Packingtown, and he faced in dread the prospect of reaching the lowest. There is a place that waits for the lowest man—the fertilizer plant!

The men would talk about it in awe-stricken whispers. Not more than one in ten had ever really tried it; the other nine had contented themselves with hearsay evidence and a peep through the door. There were some things worse than even starving to death. They would ask Jurgis if he had worked there yet, and if he meant to; and Jurgis would debate the matter with himself. As poor as they were, and making all the sacrifices that they were, would he dare to refuse any sort of work that was offered to him, be it as horrible as ever it could? Would he dare to go home and eat bread that had been earned by Ona, weak and complaining as she was, knowing that he had been given a chance, and had not the nerve to take it?—And yet he might argue that way with himself all day, and one glimpse into the fertilizer works would send him away again shuddering. He was a man, and he would do his duty; he went and made application—but surely he was not also required to hope for success!

The Fertilizer Plant

The fertilizer works of Durham's lay away from the rest of the plant. Few visitors ever saw them, and the few who did would come out looking like Dante, of whom the peasants declared that he had been into hell. To this part of the yards came all the "tankage," and the waste products of all sorts; here they dried out the bones—and in suffocating cellars where the daylight never came you might see men and women and children bending over whirling machines and sawing bits of bone into all sorts of shapes, breathing their lungs full of the fine dust, and doomed to die, every one of them, within a certain definite time. Here they made the blood into albumen, and made other foul-smelling things into things still more foul-smelling. In the corridors and caverns where it was done you might lose yourself as in the great caves of Kentucky. In the dust and the steam the electric lights would shine like far-off twinkling stars—red and blue, green and purple stars, according to the color of the mist and the brew from which it came. For the odors in these ghastly charnel houses there may be words in Lithuanian, but there are none in English. The person entering would have to summon his courage as for a cold-water plunge. He would go on like a man swimming under water; he would put his handkerchief over his face, and begin to cough and choke; and then, if he were still obstinate, he would find his head beginning to ring, and the veins in his forehead to throb, until finally he would

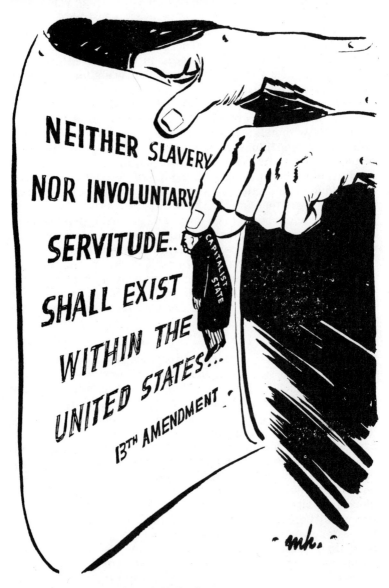

NEITHER SLAVERY
NOR INVOLUNTARY
SERVITUDE..
SHALL EXIST
WITHIN THE
UNITED STATES...
13TH AMENDMENT

CAPITALIST STATE

- mk. -

Reprinted by permission of the Weekly People.

be assailed by an overpowering blast of ammonia fumes, and would turn and run for his life, and come out half-dazed.

On top of this were the rooms where they dried the "tankage," the mass of brown stringy stuff that was left after the waste portions of the carcasses had had the lard and tallow dried out of them. This dried material they would then grind to a fine powder, and after they had mixed it up well with a mysterious but inoffensive brown rock which they brought in and ground up by the hundreds of carloads for that purpose, the substance was ready to be put into bags and sent out to the world as any one of a hundred different brands of standard bone phosphate. And then the farmer in Maine or California or Texas would buy this, at say twenty-five dollars a ton, and plant it with his corn; and for several days after the operation the fields would have a strong odor, and the farmer and his wagon and the very horses that had hauled it would all have it too. In Packington the fertilizer is pure, instead of being a flavoring, and instead of a ton or so spread out on several acres under the open sky, there are hundreds and thousands of tons of it in one building, heaped here and there in haystack piles, covering the floor several inches deep, and filling the air with a choking dust that becomes a blinding sand storm when the wind stirs.

Inhuman Labor

It was to this building that Jurgis came daily, as if dragged by an unseen hand. The month of May was an exceptionally cool one, and his secret prayers were granted; but early in June there came a record-breaking hot spell, and after that there were men wanted in the fertilizer mill.

The boss of the grinding room had come to know Jurgis by this time, and had marked him for a likely man; and so when he came to the door about two o'clock this breathless hot day, he felt a sudden spasm of pain shoot through him—the boss beckoned to him! In ten minutes more Jurgis had pulled off his coat and overshirt, and set his teeth together and gone to work. Here was one more difficulty for him to meet and conquer!

His labor took him about one minute to learn. Before him was one of the vents of the mill in which the fertilizer was being ground—crushing forth in a great brown river, with a spray of the finest dust flung forth in clouds. Jurgis was given a shovel, and along with half a dozen others it was his task to shovel this fertilizer into carts. That others were at work he knew by the sound, and by the fact that he sometimes collided with them; otherwise they might as well not have been there, for in the blinding dust storm a man could not see six feet in front of his face. When he had filled one cart he had to grope around him until another came, and if there was none on hand he continued to grope till one arrived. In five minutes he was, of course, a mass of fertilizer from head to feet; they gave him a sponge to tie over his mouth, so that he could breathe, but the sponge did not prevent his lips and eyelids from caking up with it and his ears from filling solid. He looked like a brown ghost at twilight—from hair to shoes he became the color of the building and of everything in it, and for that matter a hundred yards outside it. The building had to be left open, and when the wind blew Durham and Company lost a great deal of fertilizer.

Working in his shirtsleeves, and with the thermometer at over a hundred, the phosphates soaked in through every pore of Jurgis's skin, and in five minutes he had a headache, and in fifteen was almost dazed. The blood was pounding in his brain like an engine's throbbing; there was a frightful pain in the top of his skull, and he could hardly control his hands. Still, with the memory of his four month's siege behind him, he fought on, in a frenzy of determination; and half an hour later he began to vomit—he vomited until it seemed as if his inwards must be torn into shreds. A man could get used to the fertilizer mill, the boss said, if he would only make up his mind to it; but Jurgis now began to see that it was a question of making up his stomach.

Jurgis Endures

At the end of that day of horror, he could scarcely stand. He had to catch himself now and then, and lean against a building and get his bearings. Most of the men, when they came out, made straight for a saloon—they seemed to place fertilizer and rattlesnake poison in one class. But Jurgis was too ill to think of drinking—he could only make his way to the street and stagger on to a car. He had a sense of humor, and later on, when he became an old hand, he used to think it fun to board a street car and see what happened. Now,

---

Confessions of a Capitalist

The work of the working people, and nothing else, produces the wealth, which, by some hocus-pocus arrangement, is tranferred to me, leaving them bare. While they support me in splendid style, what do I do for them? Let the candid upholder of the present order answer, for I am not aware of doing anything for them.

Joseph Medill Patterson, *Confessions of a Drone.*

---

however, he was too ill to notice it—how people in the car began to gasp and sputter, to put their handkerchiefs to their noses, and transfix him with furious glances. Jurgis only knew that a man in front of him immediately got up and gave him a seat; and that half a minute later the two people on each side of him got up; and that in a full minute the crowded car was nearly empty—those passengers who could not get room on the platform having gotten out to walk.

Of course Jurgis had made his home a miniature fertilizer mill a minute after entering. The stuff was half an inch deep in his skin—his whole system was full of it, and it would have taken a week not merely of scrubbing, but of vigorous exercise, to get it out of him. As it was, he could be compared with nothing known to men, save that newest discovery of the savants, a substance which emits energy for an unlimited time, without being itself in the least diminished in power. He smelt so that he made all the food at the table taste, and set the whole family to vomiting; for himself it was three days before he would keep anything upon his stomach—he might wash his hands, and use a knife and fork, but were not his mouth and throat filled with the poison?

And still Jurgis stuck it out! In spite of splitting headaches he would stagger down to the plant and take up his stand once more, and begin to shovel in the blinding clouds of dust. And so at the end of the week he was a fertilizer man for life—he was able to eat again, and though his head never stopped aching, it ceased to be so bad that he could not work.

Understanding Words in Context

Readers occasionally come across words which they do not recognize. And frequently, because they do not know a word or words, they will not fully understand the passage being read. Obviously, the reader can look up an unfamiliar word in a dictionary. However, he or she can often determine the meaning simply by careful examination of the context in which it is used. A careful reader may find clues to the meaning of the word in surrounding words, ideas, and attitudes.

Below are excerpts from the viewpoints in this chapter. In each excerpt, one or two words are printed in italics. Try to determine the meaning of each word by reading the excerpt. Under each excerpt you will find four definitions for the italicized word. Choose the one that is closest to your understanding of the word.

Finally, use a dictionary to see how well you have understood the words in context. It will be helpful to discuss with others the clues which helped you decide on each word's meaning.

1. England is pre-eminent among civilized nations for the *PRODIGIOUS* development of its factory wealth and is jealously admired by foreign powers.

   PRODIGIOUS means:
   a) wasteful   c) enormous
   b) stimulating   d) limited

2. The blessings which science has bestowed on society, and the means it has still in store for *AMELIORATING* the lot of mankind, have been too little dwelt upon.

   AMELIORATING means:
   a) improving   c) harming
   b) altering   d) combining

3. As to exhaustion by the day's work, they *EVINCED* no trace of it on emerging from the mill in the evening; for they immediately began to skip about the playground.

EVINCED means:
a) denied
b) hid
c) showed
d) removed

4. It seems established by evidence that the wages of our factory workers, if prudently spent, would enable them to live in comfortable manner because of the relative *DIMINUTION* in the price of food, fuel, and lodgings.

DIMINUTION means:
a) increase
b) change
c) measurement
d) decrease

5. He was no *PROLETARIAN*: he had a stake in the country, he was permanently settled, and he stood one step higher in society than the English workman of today.

PROLETARIAN means:
a) member of the middle class
b) politician
c) rich man
d) member of the working class

6. John Stuart Mill observes that "even *DESPOTISM* does not produce its worst effects so long as individuality exists under it; and whatever crushes individuality is despotism."

DESPOTISM means:
a) rule by a tyrant
b) rule by an elected leader
c) rule by a King or Queen
d) no government at all

7. The Socialist or *ANARCHIST* who seeks to overturn present conditions is to be regarded as attacking the foundation upon which civilization itself rests.

ANARCHIST means:
a) one who wants stricter laws
b) a wealthy person
c) one who wants no government at all
d) a poor person

8. No laws, however *STRINGENT,* can make the idle industrious, the thriftless provident, or the drunken sober.

STRINGENT means:
a) lenient
b) strict
c) democratic
d) correct

Bibliography

The following bibliography deals with the subject matter of this chapter.

Thurman W. Arnold	*The Folklore of Capitalism.* Westport, CT: Greenwood, 1980.
Michel Beaud	*A History of Capitalism, 1500-1980.* New York: Monthly Review Press, 1983.
John Chamberlain	*The Roots of Capitalism.* Princeton, NJ: Van Norstrand, 1959.
Edward Greenberg	*Capitalism and the American Political Ideal.* Armonk, NY: M.E. Sharpe, 1985.
F.R. Hansen	*The Breakdown of Capitalism: A History of the Idea in Western Marxism.* London: Routledge & Kegan, 1985.
Leo Hausleiter	*The Machine Unchained: Revolution in the World Economic System from the First Steam Engine to the Crisis of Plenty.* London: Routledge & Kegan, 1933.
Friedrich August von Hayek	*Capitalism and the Historians.* Chicago: University of Chicago Press, 1954.
John Hobson	*The Evolution of Modern Capitalism: A Study of Machine Production.* London: Allen and Unwin, 1949.
Geoff Hodgson	*Capitalism, Value, and Exploitation.* New York: Basil Blackwell, 1982.
Humphrey Jennings	*1660-1886. The Coming of the Machine as Seen by Contemporary Observers.* New York: The Free Press, 1985.
David S. Landes	*The Rise of Capitalism.* New York: Macmillan, 1966.
John Lord	*Capital and Steam Power: 1750-1800.* London: Cass, 1946.
Frederick Nussbaum	*A History of the Economic Institutions of Modern Europe.* New York: F.S. Crafts and Co., 1933.
Theodore Roosevelt	*Theodore Roosevelt on Race, Riots, Reds and Crime.* New York: Sons Library, 1983.
Henri See	*Modern Capitalism: Its Origin and Evolution.* New York: N. Douglas, 1928.

3

Capitalism Today

Introduction

The capitalistic system has changed considerably in the twentieth century in the industrialized democratic nations of the world. The primary reason for this has been the ongoing transformation in the relationship between government and industry and between industry and labor. Government has been playing a larger and more visible role in the affairs of business. The proliferation of laws regulating monopolies, the pricing of goods, child labor, and minimum wage scales have succeeded in controlling or removing many of the excesses which characterized industry in the nineteenth century. Labor, for its part, has been effectively organizing. Through collective bargaining, unions have won higher wages, better working conditions, and substantial fringe benefits for their members.

As a result of these and other changes in the marketplace, the basic arguments for and against capitalism have changed to reflect contemporary conditions. While modern supporters still base their beliefs on Adam Smith's principle of laissez-faire, they have carried it a step further. Today's capitalists tend to be political conservatives who equate economic freedom with political freedom. Accordingly, many claim that when government is permitted to interfere in the economic affairs of a nation, not only will inefficiency in business result, but also an erosion of political freedom. On the reverse side, large pockets of poverty still exist in the industrialized democracies, and chronic unemployment still plagues portions of the population. These problems are offered as evidence of the failure and pending bankruptcy of capitalism. Moreover, critics of capitalism claim, even those workers enjoying a relatively high degree of affluence are small justification for the steady flow of huge corporate profits. Under the present system, it is argued, the worker never has, and never will, receive a fair share of the accrued wealth.

===

"The more economic freedom, the better."

===

The Case for Capitalism

Howard Baetjer Jr.

Howard Baetjer Jr. is on the staff of the Foundation for Economic Education (FEE), an organization that promotes the study, exploration and promotion of private ownership, free exchange, open competition and limited government. His efforts at FEE center on introducing the philosophy of freedom to students in colleges and schools. FEE believes in laissez-faire capitalism. It opposes governmental interference in economic affairs beyond the minimum necessary for maintaining peace and property rights. In the following viewpoint, Mr. Baetjer presents his case for capitalism.

As you read, consider the following questions:

1. Mr. Baetjer cites taxi licenses as an example of how regulation interrupts free enterprise. What makes his example so shocking?
2. Why is revolutionary America a good example of laissez-faire capitalism, according to the author?
3. Some people believe that in a capitalist economy, the poor get poorer and the rich get richer. What reasons does the author give that refute this assertion?

Howard Baetjer Jr., excerpted from the lecture, "In Praise of Laissez-Faire Capitalism," February 12, 1985. Reprinted with the author's permission.

My purpose is to make the case for pure capitalism. That is: minimal government, the private property order, and laissez-faire. Put another way, I want to make a case for a consistently free society, as the ideal toward which our nation should strive....

All right, what do we mean by a free society?...We mean *a society in which all peaceful, voluntary actions and interactions are permitted, and all use of force or fraud, except defensively, is forbidden:* a society in which there is no coercion—no physical force whatever—used on peaceful people. Thus it is a society marked by private ownership of property and an unregulated market. It is a laissez-faire political economy in which government functions *only* to assure justice and keep the peace.

This, we submit, is the ideal for a good society. Such a society has never existed, of course, and quite possibly it never will; certainly it will not in our lifetimes. The point, then, is that the closer we can come to achieving this ideal, the better off we will be. The more economic freedom, the better.

From the standpoint of history, it seems to some of us that it should be unnecessary to argue for a free economy. We think that people could just look at the record, and see that economic freedom works....

America's Free Enterprise

In 1776 was born the first nation founded on the principle of fundamental individual rights to life and liberty, and therefore property (on which life and liberty depend). The Founders held that rights come not from government, but from, in Jefferson's word, the "Creator." That is, rights *precede* government—they exist in the nature of things. And: "to secure these rights, governments are instituted among men." That's it—no other purpose mentioned. They saw government itself, furthermore, as the major threat to liberty; consequently the Constitution of this nation was designed to limit government very strictly. With the birth of this nation, under this philosophy, began an era of unprecedented development and improvement in the human condition.

Never before (and never since) had the quality of life improved so fast. Let me illustrate this with some figures from the Census Bureau's *Historical Statistics of the United States*.

What happened to the cost of living? Well, as more and more goods were produced in greater and greater numbers, prices of just about everything dropped. The consumer price index for 1801 is estimated at 50. In the next century it fell steadily, except in inflations around the wars, to 25 in 1901. Every dollar could buy *twice as much* as a century earlier. That is the way it is in a free economy—things get steadily cheaper.

What about employment opportunities? Well, immigrants of all kinds, many with neither money nor a word of English, were absorbed by the millions. Imagine the immigration that occurred here around the turn of the century, in the context of present-day unemployment problems, and Congressional efforts to restrict immigration for employment reasons. In 1900 our population was seventy-five million people. In the next decade, immigration alone increased that number by nearly 10%. 7.2 million people—*unemployed* people—dumped themselves on the economy. And what do you suppose unemployment for the decade averaged? Four and a half percent—well below what is known today as the "full-employment rate." Why? Because the labor markets were largely free. By the millions these people suffered through the first chaotic days or weeks, found odd jobs or work in sweatshops, then went on to better jobs, learned new skills, moved out of the cities, prospered, and sent their grandchildren (our parents, in many cases) on to opportunities they had never dreamed of. That's the way it is in a free economy—unemployment is not a problem....

The Invisible Hand of the Marketplace

In short, the time when this country was most free economically was a time of unprecedented prosperity for people of all kinds. And this was not an entirely free economy, but it was relatively free—much more free than what we have now. It was free *enough* so that able people had broad scope for creative action, not regulated at every turn like today. So that the "invisible hand" of the marketplace could direct resources to where they were most useful, according to profit, not political pull like today. So that people could get rich, and then, to get richer still, devote their accumulated capital to more productive tools and processes; not like today, when outrageous taxation makes getting rich almost impossible, and drives capital

---

Free Enterprise and Human Rights

Those who favor free enterprise are working to maintain or establish human freedom. They are on the side of the human spirit wherever efforts are being made to crush it. Those who stand for free enterprise have a noble cause, for it is the cause of freedom and of free man.

Clarence B. Carson, *The Freeman*, October 1985.

---

into consumption and useless tax shelters. So that people who conceived of mutually beneficial arrangements could put them into practice, without a license or permit or union card, like today. In short, it was free enough so that an unencumbered people could pursue happiness as each saw fit. In doing so, they made the land a better place for all. Some hundreds or thousands of the rich got richer, yes. At the same time millions and millions of the poor got richer, too. That's the way it is in a free economy....

The people of this country prospered at an unprecedented rate because and to the extent that our economy was free, our government was limited, and our property was protected.

As government has grown and intervened in the economy, our growth in prosperity has slowed accordingly. Let me illustrate.

I mentioned the dramatic decrease in the cost of living over the century of the 1800's, our most capitalistic period. The consumer price index decreased by half between 1801 and 1901. The prices of goods overall had dropped so much that dollar for dollar, everybody was twice as rich. What has happened to the dollar in the eighty years since then, especially since 1913, when the Federal Reserve System was assigned the task of "stabilizing" its value?

Well, the CPI was back up to 50 by 1919, six years after the Fed took control. It dropped again in the Depression, but by 1943 Roosevelt's exuberant spending had pushed it back up to fifty— where it had stood 142 years before. It added another 50 in 24 years, standing at 100 in 1967. The next fifty took eight years, the next four, the next less than two, and last month it stood at 315, more than six times what it had been in 1943. This is 16 cents in 1943 terms. Thank goodness the Federal Reserve "stabilized" the dollar's value....

Employment Opportunities Lessen

How about employment opportunities, especially for those without much education, skill or capital? In the days when our economy was mostly free, whenever such a person found another willing to pay him for a good or service, he was in business. But now a host of regulations, taxes, license laws, registration fees, union rules, minimum wages and other controls stand in the way. Massive unemployment and underemployment result. Take the taxicab business in New York City, for example. At the turn of the century, all some poor immigrant there had to do to get into it was beg or borrow a car, and pencil T-A-X-I on a scrap of cardboard in the window. Guess what it costs today just to get permission to go into the business? Around $60,000! That opportunity has been shut off by law.

And how about wages, which rose steadily for people at all levels of society throughout our most capitalistic period? Well, certainly wages today are higher in dollar terms than they have ever been before. But there are two important differences in this age of interventionism. The dollars won't buy as much. The other is that the government takes away a large chunk of our wages in taxes. The result of this two-pronged invasion of our property is that Americans on the whole have seen their steady growth in real wages slow, and then stop. Recently we seem to be making less....

Now don't misunderstand me. It may sound as if I have nothing good to say about American society, our economic condition, and our prospects for the future. Nothing could be farther from the truth. I recognize and bless my luck each day that with all our problems, we are the freest, most prosperous society in the world, that no society has ever lived so well. I delight in the new pleasures and marvels our fellows produce for us every day: from Steven Spielberg's movies and the American Ballet Theatre to fiber optic technology and Commodore computers at less than a hundred dollars apiece. I marvel at the resiliency of our basically market economy, hampered and obstructed though it is, which keeps generating new goods, services, jobs and profits in the face of inflation, high interest rates and the rest. Who would have expected People Express, for example, notwithstanding deregulation, to be flying us all over the country for less than it costs to take the bus? And I bow my head, in respect and gratitude, to those whose creativity, energy, and faith—in themselves and in the promise of America—continue to make these wonders possible. Despite the obstacles, they study, they save, they invest, they strive,...they produce.

A Moral and Effective System

Capitalism....recognizes several necessary conditions for the kinds of voluntary relationships it recommends. One of these presuppositions is the existence of inherent human rights, such as the right to make decisions, the right to be free, the right to hold property, and the right to exchange what one owns for something else....

Capitalism is quite simply the most moral system, the most effective system, and the most equitable system of economic exchange.

Ronald H. Nash, *Imprimis*, July 1985.

I'm not down on America. I love the place. But that just makes me want to see her potential achieved. What greater marvels, what unimagined abundance might we have if other industries were deregulated, if there were no inflation, if we didn't need permission to work in a chosen trade? I hate waste, of time, talent, and money. I share the sentiments of the beer ad: "Who says we can't have it all?" Creative people can make the world a better place to the farthest limit of human ingenuity, *if* they are free to do so. That freedom is precious. That's why I want us to get back on the track of laissez-faire.

How do we get back on the track? Well, one thing is to understand the economic principle I have been suggesting to this point: economic freedom leads to prosperity, and government intervention obstructs it....

In a free economy...all interactions are voluntary, freely chosen by those involved. And when people are free, they interact only when they have something to gain from it. This means that in a free economy, all interactions lead to mutual benefit. In place of the force and threatened harm of intervention, the free economy places free choice and mutual benefit....

Virtue of Free Economy

This is the virtue of the free economy. The whole fabric of economic interactions is freely chosen, cooperative, and generally beneficial. Each party to an exchange believes he is benefiting. This point bears emphasis because so many believe that in capitalism the rich get richer at the expense of the poor or that the seller of a good exploits the buyer, or vice versa, so that one is better off and the other worse off. When one is free to engage in a transaction or not, he does so only when he believes he will be better off for it. Think about your trips to the ice cream shop: you put your money down for the ice cream; they put down the ice cream for the money. You care for the ice cream more than you do for the money at that point, and they don't want the ice cream, they want the money. Everybody goes away content. There is a mutual "thank you" as you exchange goods and money, because you both are better off....

People ought to be free economically as well as every other way. Laissez-faire is a great system, both practically, because it works to the increasing well-being of all, and ethically, because it suits basic principles of decent interpersonal behavior. It is a system that deserves our hearty support.

"By its very nature, the capitalist system is compelled to exploit the resources and labor of society for the purpose of maximizing profits."

The Case Against Capitalism

Michael Parenti

Michael Parenti has lectured and taught at a number of universities and has written many articles and books on American politics, foreign policy and ethnic politics. In the following viewpoint, Mr. Parenti argues that capitalism is inherently exploitive. Since capitalists' main motive is to make bigger and bigger profits, they necessarily ignore humanity's needs as they make themselves richer.

As you read, consider the following questions:

1. According to the author, how are profits generated?
2. Why do the nation's economic problems, like poverty, persist, according to the author?

Adapted from DEMOCRACY FOR THE FEW, Second Edition, by Michael Parenti. Copyright © 1977 by St. Martin's Press, Inc., and used with publisher's permission.

About one-fifth of one percent of the population, the "super rich," own almost 60 percent of the corporate wealth in this country. Approximately 1.6 percent of the population own 80 percent of all stock, 100 percent of all state and municipal bonds, and 88.5 percent of corporate bonds.[1] There are sixty billionaire families in the United States and over 100,000 millionaires. In just about every major industry, be it steel, oil, aluminum or automotive, a few giant companies do from 60 to 98 percent of the business. Some two hundred companies account for about 80 percent of all resources used in manufacturing....The wealth of America is not in the hands of a broadly based "middle-class ownership." If anything, the trend continues to be toward ever greater concentrations of economic power.

Yet the public is still taught that the economy consists of a wide array of independent producers....

Objectives of Corporate Policy

In their book *Monopoly Capital*, Baran and Sweezy write: "The primary objectives of corporate policy—which are at the same time and inevitably the personal objectives of the corporate managers—are...strength, rate of growth and size....Profits provide the internal funds for expansion. Profits are the sinew and muscle of strength....As such they become the immediate, unique, unifying, quantitative aim of corporate success."[2] The function of the corporation, as corporation leaders themselves announce in their more candid moments, is not to perform public services or engage in philanthropy but to make as large a profit as possible.

The social uses of the product, its effects upon communal life, personal safety, human well-being and the natural environment, win consideration in capitalist production, if at all, only to the extent that they do not violate the pecuniary interests of the producer.

This relentless pursuit of profit results from something more than just the greed of businessmen. It is an unavoidable fact of capitalist life that enterprises must expand in order to survive. To stand still amidst growth is to decline, not only relatively but absolutely. Robert Theobald concludes that business firms

> have a special interest in the fastest possible rate of growth, which may not be compatible in the long run with the interests of society....The corporation's profits depend essentially on economic growth and...any slowing down in the rate of increase in production tends to cut into the profits of the firm. The corporation must therefore press for policies that will cause the most rapid rate of growth.[3]

Profits are made by getting workers to produce more in value than they receive in wages. Profits are accumulated in the form of savings which produce interest, or capital investments which produce further profits. Corporate profits are themselves surplus wealth which must either be distributed to the rich as dividends for their private consumption or reinvestment, or reinvested by the corporation for more profit. Capital must always be realizing itself through investment, through its actualization and expansion in labor and production. Ironically then, those with great wealth face the problem of constantly having to devise ways of making more money, of finding profitable areas into which they can invest their profits....

Corporations draw subsidies from the public treasure, rig prices at artificially high levels, impose speedups, layoffs and wage cuts, and move to cheaper labor markets in other countries. In these ways they are often able to increase profits amidst widespread want and unemployment. Business does fine but the people suffer. The economy booms but the people bust....

By cutting labor costs in order to increase profits, corporations also cut into the buying power of the very public that is supposed to buy their commodities. This is one of the contradictions of capitalist economics:

> Every capitalist's ideal would undoubtedly be to pay his workers as little as possible, while selling products to better-paid workers from other businesses. For the system as a whole, no such solution is possible; the dilemma is basic to capitalism. Wages, a cost of production, must be kept down; wages a source of consumer spending, must be kept up.[4]

The Case Against Capitalism

Far from being a machine for bringing people out of poverty, capitalism perversely condemns millions to poverty in the midst of the means sufficient for creating an abundance for all and in the midst of the obscene luxury enjoyed by the capitalist minority.

The People, September 14, 1985.

It is often claimed by businessmen that wage increases are the cause of inflation. In fact, wages have not kept pace with profit growth....It is not wage demands that determine the upward direction of prices. *The "wage-price spiral" has really been a profit-price spiral, and the worker is more the victim than the cause of inflation.*

The tendency in a capitalist economy is toward the kind of chronic instability caused by overproduction, overinvestment, underconsumption, misuse of productive capacities and labor resources, distorted growth patterns, social dislocation, a glut of nonessential consumer goods and services and a shortage of essential ones. Production is sometimes cut back, sometimes intensified, in order to maintain profits; prices are raised to compensate for diminished sales; and layoffs and wage cuts are imposed whenever possible. Demand decreases; markets shrink still further; prices are rigged still higher; inventories accumulate; investment opportunities disappear; capital—much of it nothing more than an elaborate web of credit—begins to "shrink away," and the country moves toward a recession. This instability is endemic to the system, there having been at least sixteen business cycles within the last hundred years.[5]

Recessions function to keep labor from getting "too aggressive," as well as weeding out the weaker capitalists. In boom times, with nearly full employment, workers are more ready to strike and press for better contracts. Other jobs are easy to get, and business finds it too costly to remain idle while markets are expanding. Wages are able to cut into profits during good times, but a recession reverses the trend. Business is better able to resist labor demands. A reserve army of unemployed helps to deflate wages. Unions are weakened and often broken; labor contracts offer little in the way of gains and benefits, and profits rise far faster than wages. A review of the U.S. economy for the recession year of 1975 shows big business "coming out ahead of the workers in most areas. The general pattern reveals increased profits, decreased real wages, increased unemployment, higher labor productivity and decreased strike activity."[6]

During recessions, real hardship is experienced by millions, especially those in the lower-income brackets. But the very rich, enjoying vast reserves, suffer no deprivations to speak of in their personal lives....

World's Resources Devoted to Profit

One explanation as to why our nation's economic problems remain unsolved or actually worsen is that most of the resources of our society are devoted to other things, to the production of goods and services for private profit. Those who insist that private enterprise can answer our needs seem to overlook the fact that private enterprise has no such interest, at least not in those areas where no profit is to be had. The poor may *need* shoes but they offer no market for shoes; there is a market only when need (or want) is coupled with *buying power* to become *demand*. The shoe manufacturer responds to market demand—that is, to a situation in which he can make money—and not to human need no matter how dire it be. When asked by the Citizens' Board what they were doing about the widespread hunger in the United States, numerous food manufacturers responded that the hungry poor were not their responsibility. As one company noted: "If we saw evidence of profitability, we might look into this."[7] ...

Some defenders of the established system contend that the pursuit of profit is ultimately beneficial to all since the productivity of the corporations creates mass prosperity. This argument overlooks several things: high productivity frequently *detracts* from the

Reprinted with permission.

common prosperity even while making fortunes for the few, and it not only fails to answer to certain social needs but may create new ones. The coal mining companies in Appalachia, for example, not only failed to mitigate the miseries of the people in that area; they *created* many miseries, swindling the Appalachians out of their land, underpaying them, forcing them to work under inhumane conditions, destroying their countryside and refusing to pay for any social costs resulting from corporate exploits....

The apologists for capitalism argue that the accumulation of great fortunes is a necessary condition for economic growth, for only the wealthy can provide the huge sums needed for the capitalization of new enterprises. Yet a closer look at many important industries, from railroads to atomic energy, would suggest that much of the funding has come from the public treasury—that is, from the taxpayer—and that most of the growth has come from increased sales to the public—from the pockets of consumers. It is one thing to say that large-scale production requires capital accumulation but something else to presume that the source of accumulation must be the purses of the rich.

In areas of private research giant corporations leave a good deal of the pioneering work to smaller businesses and individual entrepreneurs, holding back their own resources until money is to be made. Referring to electric appliances one General Electric vice-president noted: "I know of no original product invention, not even electric shavers or heating pads, made by any of the giant laboratories of corporations....The record of the giants is one of moving in, buying out and absorbing the small creators."

Apologists for the present system insist that big production units are more efficient than smaller ones. In fact, it is highly questionable whether the huge modern firm represents the most efficient form of production. In many instances, production units tend to become less efficient and more bureaucratized with size, and after a certain point in growth there is a diminishing return in productivity....

The power of the business class is not total, "but as near as it may be said of any human power in modern times, the large businessman controls the exigencies of life under which the community lives."[8] The giant corporations control the rate of technological development and the terms of production; they fix prices and determine the availability of livelihoods; they decide which labor markets to explore and which to abandon; they create new standards of consumption and decide the quality of goods and services; they divide earnings among labor, management and stockholders and donate funds to those political causes they deem worthy of support; they transform the environment itself, devouring its natural resources and poisoning the land, water and air; they command an enormous surplus wealth while millions live in acute want. And they exercise trustee power over religious, recreational, cultural, medical and charitable institutions and over much of the media and the educational system....

America Does Not Belong to the People

Many of us have been taught that "America belongs to the people," but in fact almost all Americans are tenants, debtors, and hired hands in their own country, working for someone else, paying rent to someone else, or paying high interest rates on mortgages, loans and installment purchases to someone else. In these relationships the advantage is on the side of the employer, the landlord, the manufacturer and the bank. The boss hires us because he can make a profit from our labor; the landlord rents to us so that he can make an income on the rental; the manufacturer sells to us because he can make more wealth on his product than he put into it; and the bank or loan company extends credit so that it can get back substantially more than it lends.[9] ...

The history of the great "affluence" in the United States since World War II is of people becoming increasingly entrapped as wage

100

earners, tenants and debtors in a high-production, high-consumption, high-profit system. Millions of Americans live under starvation conditions; millions are desperate for work; millions are afflicted by one or another socioeconomic pathology. Millions live in crowded, dilapidated, poorly ventilated, ill-heated and hazardous domiciles. Millions who identify themselves as middle class live in overpriced, poorly constructed, heavily mortgaged homes or high-rent apartments that consume a large part of their incomes while providing living quarters that are far from satisfactory. Millions are immobilized by inadequate or nonexistent public transportation facilities and have no access to decent recreational areas. Millions complain about living empty, joyless, lonely lives. At the same time, environmental devastation continues unabated: our rivers are turned into open sewers by the countless tons of raw industrial waste dumped into them by industry, our air made foul, our forests and wildlife destroyed, our roadsides uglified by commercial enterprise, and our cities are showing serious signs of decay, bankruptcy and social demoralization.

Power Held by a Few

Presiding over all this are the privileged few who control the enormous corporate wealth of the society who have more money than they know what to do with and who enjoy all the advantages of power and position that come with wealth.

It is not enough to denounce the inequities that exist between the few and the many; it is also necessary to understand the connection between them. For it is the way wealth is organized and used which creates most of the existing want. By its very nature, the capitalist system is compelled to exploit the resources and labor of society for the purpose of maximizing profits. It is this operational imperative of the system which perforce creates the commodity glut, the privation, wastage, scarcity, unemployment and general economic oppression which brings misery and malaise to so many. It is the concentrated power of corporatism which prevents a reordering of our priorities and a move toward a more equitable and sane society.

1. Ferdinand Lundberg, The Rich and the Super Rich (New York: Lyle Stuart, 1968), pp. 144 ff. Also Robert Lampman, The Share of Top Wealth-Holders in National Wealth (Princeton, NJ: Princeton University Press, 1962).

2. Baran and Sweezy, Monopoly Capital, pp. 39-40.

3. Robert Theobald, The Challenge of Abundance (New York: American Library, 1962), p. 111.

4. "Economy in Review," Dollars and Sense, March 1976, p. 3

5. David M. Gordon, "Recession Is Capitalism as Usual," New York Times Magazine, April 27, 1975.

6. Ben Bedell, "Workers Lost Out in 1975," Guardian, January 14, 1976, p. 4.

7. Quoted in Hunger, U.S.A., a report by the Citizens' Board of Inquiry into Hunger and Malnutrition in the United States (Boston: Beacon Press, 1968), p. 46.

8. Thorstein Veblen, The Theory of Business Enterprise (New York: New American Library Edition, n.d.), p. 8. Originally published in 1904.

9. A basic distinction one might make is between those who own and control the wealth and institutions of the society—the "owning class," or "propertied class"—and those who are

dependent on the owning class for their employment. The latter, the "working class," includes not only the blue-collar workers but also accountants, clerks, professors and anyone who has a job or is try to get one. The distinction is blurred somewhat by the range of wealth within both the owning and working class. Thus while "owners" include both the owners of giant corporations and the proprietors of small grocery stores, the latter control a minuscule portion of the wealth and hardly qualify as part of the *corporate* owning class. Likewise, among the working class are professionals and middle-level executives who in income and life-style tend to be inentified as "middle class," apart from "ordinary workers." Then there are some stars from the entertainment and sports worlds, some lawyers and many doctors who earn such lavish incomes that they invest their surplus wealth and become in part, or eventually in whole, members of the owning class.

"Under capitalism, job discrimination pays—literally."

Capitalism Creates Racism

The People

The People is a daily newspaper published by the Socialist Labor Party. Founded in 1891, it is one of the oldest socialist newspapers in the United States. In the following viewpoint, *The People* expresses its belief that the capitalist system encourages racism. White middle class employers hire minorities at a lower salary and thus keep them in a perpetual state of poverty. The only way to eliminate racism is to eliminate its cause—the economic system of capitalism.

As you read, consider the following questions:

1. Why does the author believe that supporters of capitalism really want to eliminate affirmative action quotas?
2. How does the author argue that racism increases private profits?
3. According to the author, how can capitalism be eliminated?

The People, "Civil Rights Axed While Racism Persists," July 20, 1985. Reprinted with permission.

Capitalist-class lackeys...claim that their accelerating attack on affirmative action and other civil rights programs is motivated by a desire to combat racism and discrimination.

They argue that race- or sex-based quotas, goals or timetables intended to promote fairness or equality of opportunity for minorities and women in housing, education, hiring, job promotion, wages and so on are inherently discriminatory.

They argue that, all things being equal, to promote opportunities for one race or sex at the expense of another race or sex is the essence of discrimination. Moreover, they assert that things *are* equal for both sexes and all races because of the "successes" of civil rights legislation and enforcement programs like affirmative action—the very measures they now seek to dismantle.

"Things," however, are hardly equal.

The plight of blacks and other minorities in the United States amply demonstrates that fact. Black adult unemployment is twice the rate for whites, and black youth unemployment is nearly triple the white rate. White families, on average, make almost double the income of black families and a third more than Hispanic families.

Increasing Inequality

Although similar conditions exist in nearly every major U.S. city and in many rural areas across the country, nowhere is racial inequality more evident than in the traditional bastion of U.S. racism, the South. According to a recent series of articles on Southern race relations in *The New York Times:*

• After two decades of political "equality," many cities and public schools in the South are more fully segregated now than they were before civil rights legislation was enacted. Thousands of whites have moved into nearly all-white suburbs—often aided in their migration by discriminatory real-estate promotions and financing schemes.

• In 1960 blacks made up only 39 percent of Atlanta's population; today they make up 67 percent. In 1970 Atlanta's schools were 35 percent white; today they are more than 90 percent black. Nearly two-thirds of all white students attend private—and nearly all-white—"academies." The same pattern of segregation is evident in all the Southern states.

• Public schools in the South are generally controlled by white superintendents and school boards—who often send their own children to the private schools. Both white- and black-controlled schools suffer from a lack of resources resulting from the conditions of poverty prevailing in black neighborhoods.

• Nearly 66 percent of all black workers in the 11 Southern states work as service workers—mostly as maids, cooks and waiters, as unskilled general laborers, or as semiskilled operators—like chauffeurs, delivery people and dressmakers. Only 32 percent of white workers work in such jobs in these states. About 59 percent of black families have incomes below $15,000 as against 31 percent of white families.

• Despite some gains in political representation in a few large cities, most state, county and city governments are still disproportionately white—due in large part to discriminatory voting regulations adopted to achieve that result.

• In the rural South, the Jim Crow segregation laws which civil rights legislation ostensibly did away with still exist in practice. In many rural Southern towns there are still bars where blacks know they cannot get a drink, motels in which they cannot get a room, restaurants in which they cannot eat, doctors' offices with segregated waiting rooms, and even city halls with segregated restrooms.

A Matched Set

The persistence of racist economic and social discrimination demonstrates that capitalism and racial oppression are inextricably bound together....

The fact is that there are basic economic factors that make racism under capitalism inevitable. The inability of capitalism to provide jobs for all workers, as well as its use of the resulting job competition to keep wages low are such factors. By further restricting educational and job opportunities for blacks and other minorities, capitalists burden those workers with a disproportionate share of unemployment and add racist fuel to the competition.

The People, February 16, 1985.

The past decade has also seen a rise in overt racism and acts of racial violence perpetrated by whites—and no end to that violence is in sight. Violent paramilitary sects like the Ku Klux Klan, the Nazis, the Aryan Nations and other fascistic white supremacist groups have become increasingly brazen in their assaults....The violence of such groups is often aided and abetted by local and other governmental authorities.

The capitalist-class elements behind the current offensive against civil rights know that "things" are not equal—that the overwhelming majority of blacks and women in this country still suffer the effects of virulent racism and sexism. Their campaign must therefore be regarded as deliberately racist and sexist.

A Capitalist Purpose

These elements are fueling racist and sexist attitudes for a purpose. That purpose is to aid the current capitalist-class offensive against workers generally—an offensive undertaken in the interest of bolstering capitalist profits in a time of increasing economic crises for world capitalism.

For, under capitalism, job discrimination pays—literally. The lower wages paid to women and minorities mean higher profits for the capitalists who exploit them. Moreover, the racist and sexist divisions and tensions discrimination fosters prevent working people from challenging the capitalists as a unified force, and the resulting competition among these various groups of workers helps hold down the wages of *all* workers.

While the campaign against civil rights must be opposed and condemned, the solution to the problem of race and sex discrimination cannot lie in simply recognizing and fighting against the added burdens that capitalism heaps on minority workers. The solution lies in a successful working-class struggle to establish a new social and economic system that cannot materially benefit from racism and sexism. For only by abolishing the class-ruled, profit-motivated capitalist system itself can we eliminate these evils and secure equality for all.

4

"One of the great merits of capitalism is that by its very nature employers are virtually compelled to be oblivious to race."

Capitalism Is the Key to Eliminating Racism

George Reisman

A long-standing indictment of capitalism has been that it perpetuates racism. If there were no government-inspired laws that insist upon the hiring of blacks, blacks would not be hired. In the following viewpoint, George Reisman argues that rather than promoting racism, a free enterprise economy actually eliminates it. Profit-seeking employers, under capitalism, are unconcerned with race. Their principle, as outlined by the author, is: "of two equally good workers, hire the one who is available for less money; of two workers available for the same money, hire the one who is the better worker." Mr. Reisman is an associate professor of economics at Pepperdine University in Malibu, California. He believes that successful employers will not indulge in racist emotions when they can hire a qualified minority for a lower salary than they would pay a white.

As you read, consider the following questions:

1. The author points out that blacks today make less money than whites. Why does he insist that capitalism is not at fault for this inequity?
2. Why does the author believe that capitalism would eliminate the need for public housing for blacks?

George Reisman, "Capitalism: The Cure for Racism." The following is excerpted from, and is reprinted by permission of, *The Intellectual Activist* (131 Fifth Avenue, New York, NY 10003).

A gross inequality exists in the United States between the economic level of the average black and that of the average white. The typical black today earns only sixty-two percent of what the average American earns.

Because the United States is viewed as a fundamentally capitalistic country, this inequality is often blamed on the nature of capitalism. And, as a result, capitalism is frequently denounced as a system of economic exploitation of blacks.

I will refute the following major accusations commonly made against capitalism. 1) Under capitalism, black workers are paid less than whites for the identical work. 2) The skills and abilities of black workers are not utilized, i.e., blacks are arbitrarily shunted into low-skilled, low-paying jobs or into unemployment. 3) Blacks must pay higher rents than whites for the same or even inferior housing, and higher prices for the same or even inferior goods.

The basis of these accusations is the illegitimate treatment of a mere historical association as though it were a fundamental, causal connection. Namely: Capitalism is associated with the history of the United States. The history of the United States is also associated with a record of injustices committed against blacks. Hence, it is concluded, capitalism is guilty of the above accusations. The conclusion is obviously a *non-sequitur*.

My theme is that the above accusations are absolutely incorrect insofar as they are levelled against capitalism; and that to the extent they are correct as descriptions of past or present conditions in the United States, the cause of the injustices is *a violation of the principles of capitalism*. Far from being the source of such injustices, capitalism is the *remedy* for them....

Capitalism and Justice for the Black Worker

Let us begin with the accusation that under capitalism blacks are paid less than whites for the identical work.

Such injustice is contrary to the operation of the profit motive, and is speedily eliminated where the profit motive is free to operate. Under the profit motive, if two kinds of labor are equally good, and one is less expensive than the other, employers choose the less expensive, because doing so cuts their costs and raises their profits. The effect of choosing the less expensive labor, however, is to *raise* wages, since it is now in greater demand; while the effect of passing by the more expensive labor is to *reduce* its wages, since it is now in lesser demand. This process goes on until the wages of the two kinds of labor are either perfectly equal or the remaining difference is so small as not to be worth caring about by anyone....

Race Is Irrelevant

Indeed, profit-seeking employers *qua* profit-seeking employers are simply unconcerned with race. Their principle is: of two equally good workers, hire the one who is available for less money; of two

108

workers available for the same money, hire the one who is the better worker. Race is simply irrelevant. Any consideration of race means extra cost and less profit; it is bad business in the literal sense of the term.

It should be realized that one of the great merits of capitalism is that by its very *nature* employers are virtually compelled to be oblivious to race. The freedom of competition under capitalism ensures this result. For even if, initially, the majority of employers were so fanatically bigoted as to be willing to forego extra profits for the sake of their prejudice, they would be powerless to prevent a minority of more rational employers from earning these extra profits. The more rational employers would thus have a relatively greater income from which to save and expand their businesses than the irrational majority. Moreover, since they operated at lower costs, they could afford to charge lower prices and thus increase their profits still further by taking customers away from the irrational majority. The results of these factors would be that the more rational employers would tend to replace the less rational ones in economic importance. They would come to set the tone of the economy, and their attitudes would be transmitted to all other employers, who would seek to emulate their success. In this way, capitalism virtually guarantees the victory of rationality over racial bigotry....

Free Enterprise Eliminates Racism

The maintenance of the general rules of private property and of capitalism have been a major source of opportunity for Negroes and have permitted them to make greater progress than they otherwise could have made. To take a more general example, the preserves of discrimination in any society...is least in those areas where there is the greatest freedom of competition.

Milton Friedman, *Capitalism and Democracy*, 1982.

It is obvious that under capitalism, if the skills and abilities of blacks are being wasted in low-skilled, low-paying jobs, it is to the financial self-interest of employers to change the situation, indeed, to seek out such blacks, and in many cases even to incur substantial costs in training them. And it follows that the greater the extent to which a black's skill or ability is wasted, the greater is the profit to be made by rectifying the situation. For example, if a black with the ability to do the work of an $80,000-a-year company vice president is working as an $8,000-a-year file clerk, it is even more to the interest of an employer to seek him out and rectify the situation than in the case of the lathe operator working as a janitor. In this case, the employer could triple the black worker's salary to

$24,000, and at the same time add $56,000 to his own profits by employing him in a capacity commensurate with his skill and ability....

The free operation of the employers' profit motive and of the wage earners' desire to increase their income would eliminate black (and white) unemployment, thus rectifying whatever non-utilization of black skills resulted from the existence of unemployment. When workers are unemployed and receiving no income, it is to their interest to offer to work for less than workers holding jobs, and it is to the interest of employers to take advantage of the situation. Because unemployed workers can be hired for less, employers are in a position to make their present workers accept lower wages, in order not to be replaced. However, as wages fall, the same total funds expended in employing labor can employ more labor. In other words, what appears to be a competition for a given number of jobs has the effect of expanding the number of jobs....

Capitalism and Justice for the Black Consumer

Laissez-faire capitalism would supply blacks with housing and all other goods on the same terms as whites. To understand why this would be so, one need only assume that it were not so, and then observe the operation of the profit motive.

Thus, as a demonstration, assume that blacks had to pay monthly rents just five percent higher than those of whites, while the landlord's costs were the same in both cases. This five percent premium would constitute a major addition to a landlord's profits. If a landlord's profit margin—his profit as a percentage of his rents—were normally ten percent, a five percent addition to his rents would constitute a fifty percent addition to his profits. Even if his profit margin were initially as high as twenty-five percent, a five percent addition to his rents would constitute a twenty percent addition to his profits.

In response to such premium rates of profit, housing construction for blacks would be stepped up, and a larger proportion of existing housing would be rented to them. The effect of this increased supply of housing, of course, would be to reduce the rental premium paid by blacks. And because a mere one percent premium would mean significant extra profits in supplying blacks with housing, even a premium of this small size could not be maintained. Thus, blacks would pay no higher rents than whites, and obtain housing equal in quality to that obtained by whites.

Likewise, assume that merchants in black neighborhoods charged higher prices than the same goods would bring in other neighborhoods, while the merchants' costs of doing business were the same in both places. The higher prices in such a case would constitute a clear addition to profits. With higher profits to be made in black neighborhoods than white neighborhoods, merchants considering the location of new stores would choose the black neighborhoods. The influx of new stores, of course, would lower selling prices in the black neighborhoods; and the process would go on until the prices and the profits to be made in those neighborhoods were no higher than elsewhere.

Capitalism and Black Progress

Operating singly and earnestly within the free enterprise system, the members of the colored race triumphed over slavery, illiteracy and discrimination in a shorter period of time than any other people in history. Owing to the ability of mankind to seize opportunities where available and to excel where merit is required, the Negro has made strides which are phenomenal, especially in view of the gauntlet that the black man has run from the seventeenth century to the present.

Judith Anne Still, *The Lincoln Review*, Fall 1984.

It is worth noting that supermarkets in particular, which are frequently criticized for charging higher prices in black areas, would be among the first to reduce their prices to the level of other neighborhoods. For the profit margins of supermarkets are normally less than two percent of their sales revenues. In the case of supermarkets, therefore, prices and profit margins only one percent higher would mean a rate of profit fifty percent higher. This would be an extremely powerful inducement to the opening of new supermarkets in black neighborhoods, and to immediate price reductions, to forestall their opening.

Blacks as Customers

Moreover, under laissez-faire capitalism racial segregation would disappear, even though it would be legally permissible on private property. It would disappear because it is fundamentally incompatible with the requirements of profitmaking and because it is irrational.

The businessman seeking profit is vitally dependent on the patronage of customers. This dependency is expressed in such popular sayings as "The customer is king" and "The customer is always right." Blacks are customers, and, as they rose economically, would be more and more important customers. It is absurd to believe that businessmen would want to turn customers away by denying them access to their premises or by humiliating them with such requirements as separate drinking fountains. The businessman's desire for profit makes him put aside all such malice. It does not matter that he personally may not like blacks. All he has to like is their money. Competition with other businessmen for the patronage of blacks then does the rest....

All of the significant injustices which blacks suffer are the result of laws representing the initiation of physical force. The solution to their sufferings is the total repeal of the mixed economy and the establishment of one hundred percent laissez-faire capitalism.

Today's intellectual establishment and today's black leaders, however, do not understand the nature of the problem. And the solution which they advocate is the further initiation of physical force. Thus, they advocate that the government compel the employment and promotion of blacks and the achievement of racial integration by force.

The Use of Force

The effect of such measures is to intensify the very problem of prejudice against blacks which they are intended to overcome. So long as there is an artificial job scarcity created by unions and minimum wage laws, the compulsory employment of blacks means the compulsory unemployment of whites. So long as blacks, for all of the reasons discussed, do tend to be less skilled, experienced and educated than whites, their compulsory promotion over whites generally means the preferment of the less able over the more able. So long as whites do not want to live on a fully integrated basis with blacks, the use of force to compel them to do so increases their fear and resentment of blacks. Thus, the use of force to counter the symptoms of prejudice places whites in a position in which they experience a conflict of interests with blacks, in which injustices are committed against them in the name of blacks, and in which they must fear and resent blacks.

Blacks, of course, are all too well aware of the hostility and resentment they encounter with every seeming success. By the nature of the means employed in their behalf, they cannot achieve what most of them want, which is to be accepted on their own merits as individuals. Indeed, as I have indicated, they must view all of their gains with the suspicion of fraud. For example, can any black today know whether he holds his job because he has earned it in fair competition with other workers, or merely because he happens to be a black and is being used as window-dressing by his employer in compliance with the requirement of filling a racial quota?...

The Most Important Step

The first and most important step in halting and then reversing the forces creating America's racial conflict is simply making it known that the conflict is the product of the mixed economy, and that the establishment of laissez-faire capitalism would achieve full justice and a harmony of the rational self-interests of all men. The mere recognition of this fact on a sufficiently wide scale would alone be enough to restore the spirit of reason to race relations. For it would give men the vision of a rational society toward which they could work by rational means....

This knowledge, that the mixed economy is the cause of our racial conflict and that capitalism is the cure, must be given the widest possible dissemination. If men understood it, it would be almost impossible for them to choose any system but capitalism. For the choice is between a system which rests on logic and reason and which holds out the prospect of a nation enjoying the harmony of men's rational self-interests, and systems which offer nothing but irrational emotion, violence and destruction. Laissez-faire capitalism is the system which deserves the support of everyone who desires justice and prosperity for all men.

If the billions lavished on mergers in the last ten years had been spent on meeting American needs,...the poor would be much fewer in number."

Capitalism Is Responsible for Unemployment

Michael Harrington

Michael Harrington is a widely respected writer, lecturer and political activist, whose books include *The Other America, Twilight of Capitalism*, and *The Vast Majority*. The following viewpoint is excerpted from his latest book, *The New American Poverty*. In it, Mr. Harrington argues that the problems of our society would end if we were to achieve full employment. He contends that while capitalists in the United States now benefit from a surplus of unemployed because they can pick and choose from a number of qualified people and hire them at a lower salary, this exploitation is immoral and should be eliminated. He believes that by making changes in our economic system and placing an emphasis on full employment and benefits for every member of our society, we could achieve a fair and equitable economy that would benefit everyone.

As you read, consider the following questions:

1. How would full employment benefit the nonpoor, according to the author?
2. What jobs does the author suggest could be created by the government?

The majority of the people of the United States cannot possibly make themselves secure unless they also help the poor. That is, the very measures that will most benefit the working people and the middle class—the rich will take care of themselves, as they always have—will also strike a blow against poverty. That is by no means an automatic process; there are specific measures that have to be worked out to deal with particular problems of the poor. But basically the programs that are in the self-interest of the majority are always in the special interest of the poor....

An increase in compassion and caring is essential, and for all of the simplifications of the early sixties, those were generous years, which does them credit. But in addition to affirming that we are indeed our sisters' and our brothers' keepers, it must also be said that the abolition of poverty requires programs—above all, full employment—that will probably do more for the nonpoor than for the poor. One is not asking men and women who have troubles enough of their own to engage in a noblesse oblige that is, in any case, patronizing. One appeals to both their decency and their interest.

Justice and Self-Interest

But how is it that justice and self-interest are, in this miraculous case, in harmony with each other?

Full employment is good for almost everyone. That is a critical reason.

In the sixties, one of the most significant accomplishments of the decade came not from the War on Poverty as such, but from the fact that unemployment declined, with one insignificant exception, in every year of the Kennedy and Johnson administrations. So it was that the working poor constituted one of the two groups (the aging were, of course, the other) who made the greatest progress in the struggle to get out of poverty. And the harmony of justice and self-interest being asserted here as a possible future was a fact then. In a mere ten years the real buying power of production workers went up by more than 15 percent....

Full Employment Motivates Work

A full-employment economy is probably more effective at job counseling than are some psychiatrists and social workers. When it becomes the norm for everyone to work, people who were "unemployable" only yesterday suddenly turn out to be quite useful. World War II demonstrated this when it took women, blacks, and the long-term unemployed and put them to work in the arms plants; so did the European postwar boom, which showed that Greek and Yugoslavian peasants could do useful work in a sophisticated West German economy. Motivation is often not a matter of individual will but of social atmosphere. Full employment motivates work....

Full employment would help a great number of the new poor; and it would benefit the nonpoor as well.

When the official figures admitted to more than eleven million unemployed and almost two million "discouraged workers" driven out of the labor market in 1983, that was obviously disastrous for those who had lost their jobs. But it also made things much worse for those who were still at work. The existence of a huge pool of idle people makes those with jobs fearful and helps drive wages down. It also sets off that vicious cycle where people clutch at every possibility and take jobs for which they are over-qualified, and those they replace do the same until the least qualified at the bottom suffer the most. As a result, a pervasive sense of insecurity saps any spirit of militancy. It was not an accident that members of the United Automobile Workers turned against concessions to the companies almost the minute the economy improved a bit in 1983. So it is that a full-employment economy would not simply help the least paid, or the unemployed; it would set in motion a virtuous cycle that would improve the lot of everyone in the labor force....

A Labor Shortage Would Eliminate Poverty

To be utterly utopian for a moment: a labor shortage in the United States would probably do more to eliminate poverty, sexism, and racism than all other policies combined....

I can hear the murmurs in the back of the hall: Fine, fine, but how do you propose to reach this promised land called full employment?

Not easily, be assured of that....

An Antisocial System

The plight of millions of children and young people in our society indicts capitalism as a thoroughly antisocial system....

Unemployment, poverty, the stresses and strains of everyday life, the resulting breakdown of the family and the resulting callous treatment of society's young—these and other social ills are the products of a system based on the private ownership of the industries and services and the exploitation of wage labor.

The People, October 12, 1985.

If America, as part of a national economic plan, decided to meet just a few of its urgent needs, it could put even more people to work in the old industrial areas. The nation, it is well known, has a rotting infrastructure of bridges, sewers, and roads. It has, precisely in the Northeast and Middle West, destroyed much of the rail system. It requires, even if OPEC's problems obscured the fact in 1983, new, environmentally benign forms of energy. These needs are, for the most part, in the public sector, but they could be supplied by both the public and private sectors. A regionally owned public rail system in the Northeast and the Midwest could, particularly if America's chaotic and antisocial subsidies for transportation were given some minimal social rationality, create jobs for people now employed in—or laid off from—steel mills and automobile factories.

And there is also that international dimension of human need....A serious transfer of funds and technology from the North to the South would create jobs in the North. The poor countries of Asia, Africa, and Latin America are not going to start tractor factories, at least in the intermediate future. They are going to buy them in the markets of the North. And just as the United States made money off the Marshall Plan—that was not the reason behind the Marshall Plan, but it was certainly one of its consequences—it could benefit if only it had the wisdom to be a bit more decent to the world's poor. And that, of course, would help the American poor as well.

The New Deal Benefited All

All of this does not add up to socialism, although that is what the demagogues of the right will say about it. But clearly all of the proposals made here are not merely compatible with the existence of a private corporate sector; they will help that sector prosper. The New Deal, it should be remembered, benefited the entire society including those who most bitterly opposed it. (In honesty I should note that in other contexts I would also cite this as one of the structural limitations and inadequacies of a New Deal that, despite my criticism, I still retrospectively support.) What is being suggested is nothing more daring than trying to allocate resources to job-generating and truly useful uses....

I would propose policies that are both "pro" corporate and a limitation on corporations. If a company makes investments in wealth-producing assets that create jobs, I would favor government support and subsidies and, if that company did those things in areas of high unemployment and poverty, generous support and subsidies. But if a company wants to move out of an area in trouble, there should be advance notice, a public determination of social, as contrasted to private, costs and benefits, a requirement that the departing corporation take financial responsibility for the social damage it does, and a loss of all tax deductions for a move that is harmful to the society. In the same spirit, there should be prohibitive interest rates on money lent for takeovers, and lower interest rates on loans for first homes and cars. (The theory and practice of differential interest rates geared to public-policy goals has operated for more than a generation in the housing sector.)

The point is, poverty cannot be abolished, and all of our other social goals cannot be accomplished, if a welfare-dependent American industry insists on getting massive subsidies for speculative investments that do not generate jobs. If the billions lavished on mergers in the last ten years had been spent on meeting

American needs, the country would be a much better place to live, the poor would be much fewer in number, and the workers and the middle class would be much better off....

Aiding the Poor

The plight of the new poor is implicated in the crisis of the world economy, that the solutions they need are the same as the solutions that are in the interest of the entire society. But there are also specific measures that relate to the new poor, and it is important to note at least a few of them here....

No "Acceptable Levels"

We believe in the absolute right of the individual to rewarding employment in a full employment economy. We reject the notion that there is an "economically acceptable level" of unemployment. Thirty years ago, the "acceptable level" was two per cent. Twenty years ago it was raised to four per cent. Five years ago, it became six to seven per cent. Today unemployment is chronically pegged at ten per cent, and to hear some wags tell it, if the current rate dips to nine per cent, that will be full employment.

To us, employment means zero unemployment, with one more job opportunity than there are workers to fill it. That's full employment.

William Winpisinger, *Socialist Review* no. 75/76.

Not only should all the benefits taken away from the working poor be restored—food stamps and Medicaid in particular—but a new principle should be adopted: No one who works full time should be poor. Full employment would have a tendency to move the labor market in that direction, by bidding up the cost of work for everyone. But the nation should not wait for this effect. The minimum wage and the various support programs should be set at levels that guarantee a nonpoverty income for every working citizen of the United States....

Moral Dimension to Helping the Poor

It is wrong...to put all of this simply in economic terms, with an emphasis on the intersecting self-interests of different groups. There is a moral dimension to the issue as well. As noted, the idealism of the sixties and the cynicism of the eighties are, in considerable measure, social products. Economics and ethics are not located in separate and sealed compartments. If there are economic policies that make moral concerns more likely, then a powerful lever for the organization of people in the battle against the new poverty is human solidarity. In the sixties, many religious people found a new relevance for their faith in the civil rights movement, in the War on Poverty, in the struggle against America's unconscionable intervention in Vietnam....

But there is reason for hope. In the sixties, the best people thought they were doing something for "them"—the blacks, the Appalachians, the truly *other* Americans. But now, more and more people are discovering that they, too, are "them." I do not mean to imply for a moment that the majority of Americans have become poor or will do so in the near future. I merely but emphatically insist that there is a growing sense of insecurity in the society, and for good reason. The very trends that have helped to create the new structure of misery for the poor are the ones that bewilder that famous middle of the American society, the traditional bastion of our complacency. And perhaps that middle will learn one of the basic lessons [I have] tried to impart: A new campaign for social decency is not simply good and moral, but is also a necessity if we are to solve the problems that bedevil not just the poor, but almost all of us.

If we do understand that point, perhaps we will do something more profound than simply to discover an enlightened self-interest. Perhaps in the process we will discover a new vision of ourselves that rises above our individual needs and unites us in a common purpose. Perhaps that pilgrimage toward the fullness of our humanity will begin once again.

"If unemployed U.S. auto workers did not insist on wages 50 per cent higher than their Japanese counterparts, there would be more jobs available in American auto factories."

Capitalism Is Not to Blame for Unemployment

John Semmens

The rate of unemployment is most often blamed on either the economy or the individual. John Semmens takes the latter view. In the following viewpoint, he contends that the rate of unemployment is artificially padded with individuals who choose not to work. John Semmens is an economist for the Arizona Department of Transportation.

As you read, consider the following questions:

1. Why does the author believe that Congress is to blame for unemployment?
2. Why does the author argue that government-created job programs are destined to fail?
3. Why would allowing free enterprise to prosper decrease unemployment, according to the author?

John Semmens, "Make-Work Won't Work," *The Freeman*, September 1983.

More and more the fate of public policy has been determined by the stampeding sacred cows. The mere mention of sacrosanct beneficiaries like the "poor," or "elderly," or "unemployed," is deemed sufficient to justify any policy, no matter how ill conceived. Objective analysis goes out the window whenever the announced *intent* of a government program is to feed a sacred cow.

The big spenders of Congress are rushing to bloat the federal deficit with "job creation" programs. Persons questioning this precipitous profligacy are characterized as heartless haters of the unemployed. With unemployment in double digits, how dare anyone delay the expenditure of funds to make work?

Tragic as an individual case of unemployment may be, sound policy cannot be made by this kind of demagogic manipulation of our emotions. We need facts about the nature of the phenomenon, its magnitude, and its causes. Without these facts no real solutions to social problems can be devised. Instead, the creation of a "crisis" atmosphere will serve as another opportunity for those holding the power to exploit productive, taxpaying businesses and individuals.

To begin with, the concept of the "unemployed" is not well defined.

Implicit in the decision of an individual whether to accept a given job is the issue of compensation. If a person turns down a job because the pay is too low he is expressing a preference for leisure at that price. Is the economy failing because it does not provide a job at the desired wage? Or is the individual to be castigated for withholding his labor?

Defining unemployment is not merely an esoteric exercise. For example, high rates of unemployment among auto workers may have a lot to do with the comparative wage costs in auto production between Japan and America. If unemployed U.S. auto workers did not insist on wages 50 per cent higher than their Japanese counterparts, there would be more jobs available in American auto factories.

Rising Expectations

Whose fault is it that some workers cannot gain the amount of compensation they desire? It is quite a common circumstance for people to be paid less than they think they are worth. If taxpayers are to be required to make up the difference between desired wage and offered wage, the destruction of productive output will be the end result.

A partial explanation for the increasing incidence of withheld labor (or unemployment) is the rising level of expectations. Legislation attempting to dictate unreasonably high wage levels has had both a direct and an indirect effect on unemployment. Decreed minimum wage laws directly prevent individuals from accepting employment at wages that would be satisfactory. The indirect effect of these decreed wages is to create unreasonable prejudices and expectations among some individuals, causing them to disdain certain kinds of employment.

The availability of alternative sources of income also supports the willingness and ability to withhold labor. The payment of unemployment compensation abets the preference for leisure among those eligible for benefits. Despite all the rhetoric about the impoverishment of the unemployed, Department of Labor statistics reveal that the average income of a family that includes at least one person drawing unemployment benefits is over $19,000. This is not pre-unemployment income. It is post-unemployment income. That is, even with one family member unemployed, the family is still bringing in income in "livable" amounts. While averages do not tell the complete story, it is clear that the so-called unemployed are not universally suffering the extraordinary deprivation that some would have us believe.

Unemployment Benefits Lavish

Even with the family income figure of $19,000, unemployment benefits are routinely denigrated as insufficient. First, the benefits are portrayed as inadequate to sustain life. Second, the idea that the provision of such inadequate benefits could actually deter someone from accepting a job is ridiculed. Despite claims of the inadequacy of unemployment benefits, research on the subject indicates that the availability of benefits does seem to affect the willingness and ability of individuals to withhold their labor from the market. In a paper presented to a "conference on the Incentive Effects of Government Spending," Princeton Professor Gary Solon disclosed that the taxation of benefits had the apparent effect of reducing the duration of unemployment by over 20 per cent.

The Ultimate Source of Wealth

Real jobs—those that produce goods and services and, in turn, create more jobs—come in only one way: by harnessing the private enterprise system, the ultimate source of all America's wealth.

Dan Dickinson, *On Principle*, July 9, 1984.

The reference point one uses to observe the national unemployment situation can influence the interpretation of the phenomenon. On the one hand, reported unemployment hovers in the double digit range. This is the worst it has been since World War II. On the other hand, 57 per cent of the adults in America have jobs. This is virtually unchanged from 15 years ago when the reported rate of unemployment was less than 4 per cent (the reputed "full" employment rate). The long term problem has not been a decline in the number of job opportunities. Rather, the problem has been that the growth of job opportunities has not kept pace with the increase in the number of persons desiring employment.

To some extent the divergence of the supply and demand for labor has been created by government intervention in the economy to fix the prices of labor above the market-clearing prices. The establishment of minimum wage laws was discussed earlier. In addition to this meddling on the lower end of the wage scale, government has raised the price of labor at the upper ends of the wage scale as well.

For blue collar occupations, governmental intervention has sanctioned the use of coercion and threats of violence as a means of extorting higher wages for union members. Intimidation of would-be labor competition is a "normal" part of the government-sanctioned collective bargaining process.

In the Professional Field, Entry Denied

For those in the professional field, the government at local, state and national levels has authorized various anticompetitive practices aimed at denying certain persons the opportunity to enter licensed or regulated professions. This has both a direct and an indirect impact on unemployment. Some individuals are directly excluded from pursuing a profession. Others, using the artificially high pay in the protected professions as a standard of reference are encouraged to withhold their labor because of unreasonably high wage expectations in general.

It should be obvious that the touted cures for unemployment being considered by Congress are totally inappropriate. Congress does not propose to deal with the issue of withheld labor. Congress does not propose to eliminate government programs that contribute to unemployment. Congress does not offer any encouragement for the economic growth that could supply many more job opportunities.

Instead, Congress pledges itself to actions based on coercion that are sure to aggravate the problem. To keep foreign firms from "stealing" U.S. jobs, Congress is considering legislation to prevent consumers from exercising free choice in their purchases. Import restrictions and domestic content laws would deny consumers the right to freely select the products most suitable to their needs. Not only will consumer satisfaction be reduced, but both the purchasing power of the dollar and eventual output per unit of input will be lowered....

To stimulate the U.S. economy Congress proposes to expend prodigious sums on public works. Men are to be put to work building roads, dams, waterways, sewers, public buildings of every sort. Of course, there is no information on how valuable these presumed public assets might be. The public sector has no means of evaluating the return-on-investment from the construction of these types of facilities.

In an abstract sense there may well be a need for roads, dams, and the like. Unfortunately, we do not know how much of these products is needed. It is possible, even likely, that many, if not most, of these public works will return only pennies on each dollar expended. The probable consequence of a massive public works program is the malinvestment of scarce capital resources. Since it requires capital to sustain employment opportunities, the malinvestment of billions of capital will inexorably reduce future employment.

Government Programs Create More Unemployment

Real wage rates can rise only to the extent that, other things being equal, capital becomes more plentiful. If the government or the unions succeed in enforcing wage rates which are higher than those the unhampered market would have determined, the supply of labor exceeds the demand for labor. Institutional unemployment emerges.

Firmly committed to the principles of interventionism, governments try to check this undesired result of their interference by resorting to those measures which are nowadays called full-employment policy: unemployment doles, arbitration of labor disputes, public works by means of lavish public spending, inflation and credit expansion. All these remedies are worse than the evil they are designed to remove.

Ludwig von Mises, *The Freeman*, February 1985.

To alleviate the plight of displaced workers and the ''hard core'' unemployed, Congress is wont to enact job-training programs. On a theoretical basis, we'd be led to predict that this would be an inefficient means of preparing people for jobs. Bureaucracies lack the economic incentive structure to effectively provide appropriate training. The past experience of the government in this area bears out the theoretical prediction.

The Comprehensive Employment and Training Act (CETA) was notoriously ineffective in training the unemployed for work. A majority of the participants in CETA never obtained productive employment as a result of their job training. Government job-training programs are a waste of time and money. Human talent that might otherwise be constructively employed will be wasted in misguided and futile efforts. Money to fund this activity will be diverted from the productive sector. This will decrease employment and output in this sector....

Government programs to create jobs by seizing and spending more resources are precisely the wrong cure for unemployment. Government spending has been increasing at a faster rate than inflation. Since the 1975 recession, federal spending has risen 50 per cent faster than inflation. If government spending really stimulates the economy, shouldn't unemployment be getting lower? The fact that government spending has not had this effect points out the precarious predicament of the predatory society.

In contrast, even the slightest moderation of government rapacity would pay big dividends. For example, let us suppose that the rate of growth of government spending had been held to match the rate of inflation over some recent time period. What would have been the employment impact of such a policy? What if the government had responded to the 1975 recession by moderating its consumption of private sector resources in this fashion?

The cumulative effect of such a policy could have been quite dramatic. The compound creation of capital invested at an average rate of return could have enabled our economy to accumulate over $600 billion more resources than presently exists. This additional capital could support an additional 5½ million job opportunities....

Stop Government Interference

What America needs is a simple program to promote economic growth. The role of government in this program is to stop interfering with voluntary productive activity. Regulations like minimum wages should be removed. Sanction of coercive collective bargaining should be repealed. Restraints on trade should be abolished. Subsidies to the inefficient should cease. Grants of monopoly must be rescinded. Laws against victimless crimes in voluntary exchange between consenting adults must be dispensed with. Finally, the bloated budgets of government at all levels have to be trimmed.

Returning resources to the private, productive sector will do more to alleviate unemployment and poverty than any other policy available to government. The wealth and well-being of ourselves and future generations hang in the balance.

Distinguishing Bias from Reason

The subject of capitalism often generates great emotional responses in people. When dealing with such a highly controversial subject, many will allow their feelings to dominate their powers of reason. Thus, one of the most important critical thinking skills is the ability to distinguish between opinions based upon emotion or bias and conclusions based upon a rational consideration of the facts.

Most of the following statements are taken from the viewpoints in this chapter. The rest are taken from other sources. Consider each statement carefully. *Mark R for any statement you believe is based on reason or a rational consideration of the facts. Mark B for any statement you believe is based on bias, prejudice, or emotion. Mark I for any statement you think is impossible to judge.*

If you are doing this activity as a member of a class or group, compare your answers with those of other class or group members. Be able to explain your answers. You may discover that others will come to different conclusions than you. Listening to the reasons others present for their answers may give you valuable insights in distinguishing between bias and reason.

If you are reading this book alone, ask others if they agree with your answers. You will find this interaction very valuable.

R = *a statement based upon reason*
B = *a statement based upon bias*
I = *a statement impossible to judge*

1. The more economic freedom, the better.
2. A purely capitalistic society has never existed.
3. In 1776 the first nation was founded on the principle of fundamental individual right to life and liberty.
4. In a free economy, consumer goods get cheaper to buy.
5. During the early 1900s, the American economy absorbed millions of immigrants into the workforce.
6. By its very nature, the system of capitalism must exploit the worker in order to make more profits.
7. The fact that about one-fifth of one percent of the population owns almost sixty percent of the corporate wealth in this country proves capitalism is not working.
8. Profits are made by getting workers to produce more in value than they receive in wages.
9. Every capitalist's ideal would undoubtedly be to pay his workers as little as possible.
10. During recessions, real hardship is experienced by millions, especially those in the lower-income brackets. But the rich, enjoying vast reserves, suffer few deprivations.
11. The boss hires us because he can make a profit from our labor; the landlord rents to us so that he can make an income on the rental; America does not belong to the people but to a handful of influential profit-makers.
12. The typical black today earns only sixty-two percent of what the average American earns, creating a gross inequality between the economic level of the average black and that of the average white.
13. Profit-seeking employers are unconcerned with race. Any consideration of race means extra cost and less profit.
14. One of the great merits of capitalism is that by its very nature employers are virtually compelled to be oblivious to race.
15. The fact that capitalists hire blacks at lower salaries then they would pay whites perpetuates inequality and racism.
16. A capitalist economy should be based on equal opportunity.
17. A labor shortage in the United States would probably do more to eliminate poverty, sexism, and racism than all other policies combined.

Bibliography

The following bibliography deals with the subject matter of this chapter.

Kenneth D. Boulding — "Driven by Rage to Accumulate," *The New York Times Book Review*, October 20, 1985.

Sam Bowles, David M. Gordon, and Thomas E. Weisskopf — "Higher Wages Will Help Productivity," *In These Times*, June 27/July 10, 1984.

Milton Friedman et al. — *Politics and Tyranny*. San Francisco: Pacific Institute for Public Policy Research, October 1985.

George Gilder — *Wealth and Poverty*. New York: Basic Books, Inc., 1981.

Brian Griffiths — "Christianity and Capitalism," *Catholicism in Crisis*, October 1984.

Michel T. Halbouty — "The Hostile Takeover of Free Enterprise," *Vital Speeches of the Day*, August 1, 1985.

Robert L. Heilbroner — "The Nature and Logic of Capitalism," *The New Republic*, October 28, 1985.

Robert L. Heilbroner — "The Future of Capitalism," *Current*, February 1983.

Paul Johnson — *Will Capitalism Survive?* Washington, DC: Ethics and Public Policy Center of Georgetown, 1979.

Robert Kuttner — "Social Equity Can Be Good Economics," *The New York Times*, September 1, 1984.

Tod Lindberg — "Four Cheers for Capitalism," *Commentary*, April 1985.

The New Republic — "Creeping Capitalism," September 16 & 23, 1985.

Joseph Nocera — "Making Capitalism Moral," *The Washington Monthly*, September 1985.

Frances Fox Piven and Richard A. Cloward — *The New Class War*. New York: Pantheon Books, Random House, 1981.

William Raspberry — "Job Picture: Blacks Are Left Out, But No One Tells Us Why," *Los Angeles Times*, March 19, 1985.

Dean Russell — "Free Markets and Human Freedom," *The Freeman*, March 1985.

The Future of Capitalism

Introduction

Ever since capitalism became the dominant economic system in Western Europe, critics have been predicting its downfall. In the last century, Karl Marx wrote that within itself capitalism held "the seeds of its own destruction." While many since that time have argued that the demise of capitalism in the Western world is imminent, it seems safe to say that it is firmly entrenched and is unlikely to disappear within the next century.

In the Third World, however, capitalism's future is much less certain. A variety of economic systems exist, including capitalism. But because this capitalist activity is primarily generated by the Western democracies through corporations based in the Third World, it is associated with the negative and repressive era of Western colonialism. Do multinational corporations help or hinder the economic and social development of the Third World? Many believe these corporations drain the underdeveloped nations of already scarce resources and grossly underpay the native workers. Others believe they provide regular work where work is desperately needed, and that while wages are low compared to the United States and Europe, they are much higher than could otherwise be found in the underdeveloped countries.

Capitalists also argue that multinational corporations educate the Third World to the ways of free enterprise, claiming capitalism will foster more productive economies. Western industrialized nations, they say, can pull the Third World out of debt not through massive handouts of aid, but by altering their economic systems. Opponents believe this to be empty rhetoric aimed at disguising the true intent of the multinationals, namely to loot and exploit. The viewpoints in this chapter address these issues. Significantly, much of capitalism's future may hinge upon its acceptance or rejection in the underdeveloped, emergent nations of the world.

"Democratic capitalism, for all its complications and imperfections, is the Third World's greatest hope for sustainable economic development."

Capitalism Can Aid the Third World

Lewis A. Engman

Lewis A. Engman was formerly chairman of the Federal Trade Commission, president of the Pharmaceutical Manufacturers Association, and assistant director of the White House Domestic Council. He holds an economics degree from Michigan, a law degree from Harvard, and studied at the London School of Economics. In the following viewpoint, Mr. Engman argues that multinational corporations, given hospitable business conditions, have shown that they can accelerate a poor country's transition to better living standards by acting as democratic capitalist transplants. By allowing corporations to flourish in the Third World, these countries will begin to notice the benefits of capitalism and decide to adopt the system as their own.

As you read, consider the following questions:

1. What reasons does the author give to support his claim that capitalism is the best system for the Third World?
2. The author gives reasons as to why authoritarianism is the worst system for Third World development. What are those reasons?

Lewis A. Engman, "How Multinational Companies Can Roll Back Third-World Poverty," *Imprimis*, March 1985. Reprinted by permission from *Imprimis*, the monthly journal of Hillsdale College, featuring presentations at Hillsdale's Center for Constructive Alternatives and at its Shavano Institute for National Leadership.

Democratic capitalism, for all its complications and imperfections, is the Third World's greatest hope for sustainable economic development. The multinational corporation is perhaps the most effective means of securing the benefits of democratic capitalism for Third-World countries. Those are the two propositions I want to establish.

Simply defined, democratic capitalism is an economic system that:
—respects private property, including intellectual property;
—welcomes all competitors;
—encourages the widest possible range of consumer choice;
—recognizes that firms, like individuals, act in their own best interest in the competitive economic process, and that the success of each participant *enriches* rather than impoverishes all others; and
—is open across borders, reflecting the reality that ours is truly a world economy.

The genius of democratic capitalism is that it is self-energizing. The system is very good at translating public will into public benefits through the agency of private interests. The freely given labors of individuals seeking to better themselves are harnessed through the mechanism of the competitive marketplace and efficiently deployed in the production of those goods and services to which society attaches greatest value.

Greed Can Work

Some have called this system immoral because it is propelled forward by greed. But the openly expressed desire to improve one's circumstances is what economic development is all about. And in a free-market economy, the only way for the individual to improve his circumstances is by providing what his fellow citizens want. If acting morally means acting in the interests of one's fellow citizens, then democratic capitalism must be the most moral of systems.

In addition to being moral, the system offers another plus: it works. During the past century, democratic capitalism has generated more development, more innovation, and more wealth than all other systems combined have produced in the history of mankind.

Authoritarian economic systems, by contrast, work far less well. Motivation is a problem. Workers whose wages are set by the state have little incentive to put forth superior effort. This is nowhere more evident than in the Soviet Union, where agricultural productivity on the private plots citizens are permitted to farm in their spare time is 30 times the productivity of the collective farms.

Innovation, too, is a problem in state-run economies. Individuals whose welfare is not tied to the economic success of the enterprises in which they work are not likely to look for ways to ensure that success. Imagination and invention are the work of a relative few.

New ideas are subject to approval by the state. The consumer has little voice in determining the rate or direction of innovation. He stands in line and counts himself lucky if the shelf is not bare....

The Frustration of Inequality

In terms of human capital and economic infrastructure, most developing countries are many decades behind the West. They cannot expect to eliminate this gap in a few years. But it is folly to equate lingering relative disadvantage with failure. The meaningful measure of economic progress is change in absolute terms.

There are today, even in this country, people who do not accept this, people who count themselves poor because they are forced to live with a black and white TV, a six-year-old car and a weekly rent obligation. By the standards of their parents or their contemporary counterparts elsewhere in the world they are rich. But they feel poor because they measure material well-being not against past circumstances but against the circumstances of others.

In some, the perception that they are less well-off than others kindles the fire of ambition and enterprise. In others, it breeds resentment and the demand that wealth be forcibly transferred from others to themselves.

Corporations and the Developing World

A quiet revolution is taking place in the relationship between multinational corporations and the developing world—they are learning to live together and like it....

Despite much publicized conflicts, multinational corporations are becoming more sensitive to the political and social needs of the third world, while, at the same time, developing countries are demonstrating greater pragmatism and confidence in their negotiations with foreign firms.

Isaiah Frank, *The Christian Science Monitor*, July 10, 1981.

The same sentiments are heard in developing nations. Many of them have experienced vast improvement in their standards of living: huts to apartment blocks, buckets to running water. But because they have simultaneously been exposed to standards of living in more developed countries, these gains are little appreciated....

Equality of Opportunity

The only equality promised by democratic capitalism is the equality of opportunity. For that our forefathers in this country fought and died. But nowhere in the orthodoxy of democratic capitalism is equality of circumstances promised. Indeed, the two concepts are philosophically contradictory.

What democratic capitalism promises is that each individual be free to improve his circumstances to the best of his ability. And the record shows that individuals, given this freedom, will advance their circumstances more rapidly and farther than they will under any other system.

Might not there be some other system in which rapid growth and development are more compatible with equality of wealth? There might be. *But no one has found it yet.*

Let's look now at the way this frustration at inequality, and the resulting efforts at redistributive solutions, tend to operate most harshly against the one institution best equipped to narrow the gap between "haves" and "have nots" in the Third World—namely, the multinational firm.

Transplanting Democratic Capitalism

As we know, the smooth operation of democratic capitalism requires certain preconditions that cannot be created overnight. It depends on values such as respect for individual rights and private property, and on basic economic infrastructures for capital formation, distribution of goods, and dissemination of market information.

These preconditions took generations to be satisfied in the developed nations where democratic capitalism is the reigning orthodoxy. And they will take decades to develop in the Third World, too, if the countries that make up the Third World are left to their own devices.

But the Third World lacks time. Its people and its leaders are in a hurry. Which is one reason, as I say, so many opt for the short-sighted shortcut of state controls.

Fortunately, there is a better alternative. Democratic capitalism does not have to be achieved in the Third World from the ground up over centuries as was the case in the West. Democratic capitalism, or many of its vital aspects, can be transplanted in almost turn-key form from places where it already flourishes. The agency of the transplant is the multinational corporation.

To the economically prostrate, administratively chaotic and philosophically adrift Third-World nation seeking to get a grasp on its future, the entry of a multinational corporation is analogous to laying sod on the desert.

Initial benefits are localized. But as the roots sink and the lessons and know-how radiate outward from the transplant, so will the benefits spread. The more transplants made, the more rapid will be the progress.

But like sod, or transplants of any sort, multinational corporations, in order to flourish and spread the benefits of democratic capitalism, require the hospitality of the host. Sod laid upon concrete quickly dries and withers. Multinational corporations deprived of the freedoms and incentives that energize their activities cease to confer benefits, and eventually withdraw whence they came.

In much of the Third World today, the multinational corporation often encounters not hospitality but hostility. This hostility, taking the form of punitive regulations, is disastrously counter-productive.

The most effective, and potentially by far the largest form of assistance for the developing world is private-sector direct investment.

No other form of assistance can compare to private-sector investment in its contribution to recipient nations. It brings with it capital, training, local job creation, tax revenues and foreign exchange earnings. In one stroke, the private firm that invests in a developing nation confers benefits it would take decades to generate locally. And these benefits, unlike the aid dollars that seep quickly into the sand, are permanent.

Capitalism Wins

The creativity of the free enterprise system has been central to the most positive industrialization and economic growth. Whenever countries of comparable resources have run the race together— Austria and Czechoslovakia, West and East Germany, South and North Korea—the economy with a significant private sector clearly has done more in fulfilling the economic aspirations of its people than has its statist counterpart. This is a matter of record.

Richard S. Williamson, *Human Events*, October 20, 1984.

Moreover, direct investment produces secondary and tertiary benefits by supporting local suppliers and satellite industries.

I have seen the transforming effect direct investment can have on the local economy in a developing country, so I am always astonished when I hear companies that make such investments vilified as being exploitative.

Biting the Hand...

Typically, a company comes in, spends millions of dollars to construct a plant, trains a work force, boosts the local economy, and produces a product that previously the host country had to import. Then when it decides to invest a portion of its local earnings elsewhere one hears it charged that the company is being exploitative.

That is ridiculous. The company has done nothing but good. And the reason it has done so is that it has invested its resources productively. If the host country wishes the profits from those investments reinvested locally, it is up to the host country to ensure that new investments will continue to be equally attractive. That is the way democratic capitalism works. If capital is not free to flow toward the promise of better yield, the system cannot produce the rapid growth and development that is its hallmark. Unfortunately, this is not always appreciated.

Take as an example the multinational pharmaceutical companies. Those firms make the highest quality medicines available in the developing world. And they produce many of them locally. They hire locally and they train the people they hire, providing them skills and know-how they could get nowhere else. In the context of most Third-World economies they are Triple-A economic citizens, a class act.

Yet the pharmaceutical industry is constantly under assault. Once its facilities are in place, developing nations often pursue policies both in their own countries and through such groups as the U.N. Conference on Trade, Aid, and Development, which have the effect of undermining the preconditions for democratic capitalism, and thus of ensuring that future direct investments in their economies will not be made....

If you are poor and yearn to be rich, it does not make sense to attack or disadvantage the rich who seek to join with you and share their wealth and their know-how. To do so under the banner of equality is to ensure that you will be neither equal nor rich....

Capitalism Created Wealth

If democratic capitalism is associated with the unequal distribution of wealth, it is because democratic capitalism, and the industrial revolution it spawned, *created* most of the world's wealth.

In pre-industrial societies, the king and a few nobles may have sat on piles of gold. But outside the castle moats it was a different story. A chair, a bowl and a hoe were the peasant's dowry. This one might have two bowls, or that one two hoes, but by and large, an equilibrium of poverty prevailed. And one is free to assume, if one wants, that it was a world free of envy and full of bliss.

Democratic capitalism changed all that. In a few centuries it heaped upon the citizens of Europe and North America a thousand times the wealth man had known in all prior history. In recent decades it has begun doing the same for dozens of other countries elsewhere in the world—and can continue doing so if permitted.

But by its nature democratic capitalism has heaped more wealth on some individuals and countries than on others. No longer is there an equilibrium of poverty. Instead, there has come to be an inequality of wealth. Is this incredibly fecund new system good because it produced wealth, or bad because it has produced inequality? I'll leave that one to the philosophers. But I will tell you this: if any of you would like to turn back the clock, I can tell you where you can go in the developing world to find people who still live in almost perfect equality. And most of them still have just a bowl and a hoe.

*"For the people of the Third World,
growth is not necessarily development and
industrialization is not necessarily salvation."*

Multinational Corporations Exploit the Third World

James W. Russell

James W. Russell teaches sociology and Latin American studies
at Lewis and Clark College in Portland, Oregon. In the following
viewpoint, Mr. Russell focuses on multinational corporations in
Mexico to substantiate his claim that they are exploitive and oppressive. He documents the way in which these corporations treat
their employees inhumanely, managing to avoid making even
minor improvements in pay, hours worked, or health benefits.

As you read, consider the following questions:

1. How do US corporations avoid improving working conditions, according to the author?
2. How does the author argue that multinational corporations
   in Mexico harm the US economy?
3. Why does the author believe that Third World employees
   tolerate this inhumane treatment?

James W. Russell, "A Borderline Case: The Sweatshops Cross the Rio Grande," *The Progressive*, April 1984. Reprinted by permission from *The Progressive*, 409 East Main Street,
Madison, Wisconsin 53703. Copyright © 1984, The Progressive, Inc.

The Third World and the First World meet on Juárez Avenue, a strip of bars, restaurants, and curio shops catering to tourists who spill over the border from El Paso. For Americans who want to photograph, purchase, or eat a bit of Mexicana, Ciudad Juárez is a convenient sally. They drive in, soak up the ambience around the "mariachi plaza," and go home.

But there is a permanent American presence in Ciudad Juárez, invisible to the sightseers though manifest to the city's inhabitants. To see it, one must take a frustrating drive through streets choked by traffic, bus fumes, and food vendors. On the outskirts of the city, in the barren Chihuahua desert, it rises like a gleaming mirage: row upon row of modern buildings and well-manicured lawns.

The buildings are *maquiladoras*, assembly plants run by foreign-based multinational corporations, most of which are headquartered in the United States. Juárez is home to about 125 foreign-owned factories that employ 45,000 people—a manufacturing nexus larger than Youngstown, Ohio, in its steel-producing heyday. Most of the *maquiladoras* operate within spanking new industrial parks, where security is tight and rent is cheap.

U.S. companies import American parts into Mexico, assemble the parts in *maquiladoras*, and export the products back to the United States. The finished goods are usually stamped, ASSEMBLED IN MEXICO OF U.S. MATERIALS. A host of U.S. corporate giants— including General Electric, Zenith, RCA, and General Motors—as well as many smaller subcontractors have set up shop along the 2,000-mile Mexican frontier, dominating the economies of such cities as Juárez, Tijuana, and Mexicali.

The companies have turned the border zone into a terminal on their global production line. More than 70 per cent of *maquiladora* work involves electronics or apparel, both product lines that require intensive labor for final assembly. U.S. companies farm out, or "outsource," the fabrication work to Mexico to save on labor costs.

If the day trippers from the United States bring dollars and leave with knickknacks, the multinational employers bring capital and leave with ready profits—superprofits, in fact, derived from superexploitation.

A Tremendous Boon

Maquiladora managers prefer to hire teen-aged women, believing them to be more dexterous and tractable than men. Since electronics assembly must be done in a clean, temperature-controlled environment, the new factories are air-conditioned, to protect the parts, not the workers, from sweltering desert heat that can send the mercury to 114 degrees. Garment manufacturers do not have that concern, so many of their factories are scattered about Juárez in old, uncooled buildings.

The *maquiladoras* are a tremendous boon to the corporations.

Ollie Harrington for the *Daily World*.

Labor costs generally run 20 to 25 per cent of what they would be in the United States; the work week is 25 per cent longer; the pace of work is faster, and Mexico's high unemployment rate disciplines the labor force. Richard Michel, who manages General Electric's seven *maquiladoras* in Mexico, boasts of a 2 per cent absentee rate in his factories, compared with 5 to 9 per cent in the United States. Productivity, he adds, is 10 to 15 per cent higher south of the Rio Grande.

Though *maquiladora* wages lag far behind those in the United

States and represent a fraction of the workers' productive output, the pay is good by Mexican standards. However, border-zone wages are declining in real terms because of unfavorable exchange rates with the dollar. U.S. prices affect Mexican prices; moreover, the workers spend between a third and half of their earnings on the U.S. side.

Gustavo de la Rosa, a lawyer who specializes in *maquiladora* workers' cases, found that the government's peso devaluations have markedly reduced real pay in Juárez: In February 1981, 80 per cent of the *maquiladora* employees were taking home the equivalent of $9.19 a day; one year later, take-home pay had slipped to $8.00; by late 1983, it had shrunk to $6.80....

Escaping Labor Laws

The *maquiladoras* run smoothly, but not because the interests of the workers are protected. Between 1971 and 1978, the government's Board of Arbitration issued 482 judgments involving *maquiladora* employees. Only fourteen were favorable to the workers.

Mexican law requires that senior workers be assured job security, but there are many ways for multinational corporations to get around the requirement. Employers can slash hours or shut the plant down for a period, thereby forcing the employees to seek work elsewhere. Companies have also been known to swap workers, eliminating accrued seniority in the process. High turnover is seen as a key to high productivity, and workers are pressured to leave when they reach their late twenties.

The border cities were opened to *maquiladora* exploitation in 1965 with the inauguration of the Border Industrialization Program. A year earlier, the Bracero Program, which provided U.S. growers with seasonal armies of unorganized Mexicans, had been canceled. President Gustavo Diaz Ordaz was facing skyrocketing unemployment in the border region—and rising unrest.

In fact, guerrilla warfare had erupted in Chihuahua. Arturo Gamiz, a rural school teacher, had organized a base of guerrillas to combat fraudulent land reform, fight the sale of forest and mineral concessions to corporations, and defend the Tarahumara Indians. The Mexican Army engaged Gamiz and his followers in battle on September 23, 1965. Most of the guerrillas were killed, and their bodies were thrown into a common grave.

Free Trade Zone Opened

The Mexican government sensed that tensions in the border area would exacerbate as growing numbers of impoverished peasants left the land and filled the already swollen ranks of the urban unemployed. So Diaz Ordaz designated the frontier region a free-trade zone, waived import duties, and granted tax breaks to the U.S.-based multinational companies.

This bonanza came at an opportune time for U.S. corporations.

140

After a long period of unbridled expansion, they were facing heightened competition from Japan, West Germany, and other nations. As foreign garment and electronics manufacturers began making inroads into the U.S. market, labor costs became a vital factor in maintaining a competitive edge. U.S. multinational companies started shifting production to such cheap labor suppliers as South Korea, Taiwan, Singapore, and the Mexican border zone.

In choosing a Third World outpost, business executives consider three variables: labor costs, freedom of operations, and stability. Even before the Bracero Program ended, Mexico's border cities suffered unemployment rates of 30 to 40 per cent; wages, following the law of supply and demand, were accordingly low. The unemployment rate in the region remains at least 40 per cent today.

A Sizable Advantage

The global corporations have devastated communities in the developing countries by shutting down dozens of plants when more profitable investment opportunities appeared elsewhere. As unions have increasingly learned in recent years, strikes against large corporations by workers in one country alone can be rapidly undermined by corporate shifts of capital to workplaces abroad where workers labour at similar levels of productivity for substantially less pay.

For the Third World, the growth of global corporations has meant more consumer goods for the rich, but deepening poverty for the majority of the people.

Transnationals Information Exchange, *Meeting the Corporate Challenge*, Report 18/19.

The Border Industrialization Program ensured multinational corporations absolute freedom. The Mexican government absolved them of tax obligations, and the U.S. Government molded the U.S. tariff code to the companies' advantage. Two provisions pegged customs duties on *maquiladora* products to the low wages paid in Mexico, not to the value added to the materials in the production process.

The PRI, which exercises firm control over Mexican affairs, has coopted most of the popular movements, including the unions, and brutally suppressed the rest. It simply rigged the 1983 state elections: "Privately, PRI officials admit that votes were manipulated," *U.S. News & World Report* noted, "because 'it was too dangerous to lose elections during a major economic crisis.' "

Attractive Options for Corporations

Cheap labor, freedom from regulation, and political stability have conspired to bring U.S. multinational corporations across the border. The total number of *maquiladoras* grew from twelve in 1965 to more than 600 by 1980.

The border zone is hardly unique: It competes with similar corporate havens in Asia and in other parts of Latin America. But the Mexican frontier has a special selling point—the "twin plant" concept. A firm can maintain its capital-intensive operations in the United States and meet its labor-intensive needs a short distance away. For example, U.S. workers can cut cloth—a task that is relatively skilled and requires major capital investment—and *maquiladora* employees can then sew it.

Runaway plants deprive U.S. workers of jobs, and the *maquiladora* competition drives down wages in the United States, particularly along the border, where there is a palpable threat that more shops will flee to Mexico.

The damage north of the border has not been offset by benefits to the south. Unemployment in Mexico's frontier area has not been reduced, and living conditions have remained, at best, unchanged. The assembly plants have become magnets for displaced peasants; local newspapers warn that 100 families a day are moving into Juárez. A marginalized, "surplus" population lives in cardboard shacks and feeds its young by begging or selling items scavenged from American parks, alleys, and dumps. Some of the poor become servants on the U.S. side; a full-time, resident maid in El Paso earns $30 to $40 a week.

The movement of women into the *maquiladoras* has strained traditional sex roles. Family strife has increased, and the idled men often turn to alcohol or crime. Many abandon their families to take jobs as undocumented workers in the United States. Spanish-language radio and television stations in El Paso and Juárez regularly broadcast appeals from wives searching for runaway husbands....

Desperation Keeps Workers Mute

Desperation is what keeps the workers mute. Challenges to the system are few. The official unions enroll only a quarter of the work force, and seem to do little more than maintain discipline for the employers. The independent unions, which are more militant than the major labor groups, have yet to make significant inroads into the *maquiladoras*.

Opposition to the system is most visible among the squatter organizations, such as the CDP, and among the leftist electoral parties. A new and important component of the opposition is the Catholic lay communities.

As in the rest of Latin America, the currents of liberation theology flow through Juárez. When the 1979 Puebla Conference of the Latin American Church called for a Christian-based community movement to raise the social and political consciousness of the poor, a number of churches in Juárez responded.

One of them was Father Oscar Enriquez's parish in the working-

142

class *colonia* of Alta Vista. From his church, Enriquez can see across the Rio Grande into the United States. He can also see the smoke of ASARCO's copper smelter as it poisons both sides of the border with lead and other toxic chemicals. Enriquez has become a leader of the Christian community movement, which now encompasses about seventy groups, with ten to fifteen members in each, that meet weekly to discuss social and political issues. The study groups have been growing, fostering a healthy skepticism toward capital among Juárez's citizens.

But even as the skepticism builds, new *maquiladoras* rise against the desert sky—concrete reminders that for the people of the Third World, growth is not necessarily development and industrialization is not necessarily salvation. If a tag could be placed on the profits of the corporate giants who have plants along the border strip, it might read, ASSEMBLED IN THE U.S. OF MEXICAN LABOR.

"Apartheid in South Africa has long had the tacit approval and overt material support of U.S. capitalism."

Capitalist Corporations in South Africa Support the White Regime

The People

The US has had business interests in South Africa since the late nineteenth century. In the past ten years, these interests have been a source of contention. Many believe US corporations support the discriminatory and oppressive apartheid regime, making change for South Africa's blacks virtually impossible. Others believe US corporations are catalysts for change, and have been almost solely responsible for the small improvements in black human rights. In the following viewpoint, *The People*, a daily socialist newspaper, condemns US economic involvement in South Africa. The author argues that US capitalist interests in the country are exploitive.

As you read, consider the following questions:

1. According to the author, how does the system of capitalism promote racism and discrimination?
2. How does the US benefit from apartheid, according to the author?
3. The author believes that capitalism must be destroyed to facilitate change in South Africa. What system is recommended to replace it?

The People, "U.S. Capitalism Bolsters Vicious Apartheid Regime," April 13, 1985. Reprinted with permission.

The struggles of long-oppressed people in southern Africa against imperialism and racism have captured attention throughout the world. And while those struggles have spread to many parts of the vast African continent, nowhere are the forces and issues more compressed than in the racist fortress of South Africa.

No American worker can look to South Africa without noting that U.S. capitalism stands side by side with the most reactionary forces in that benighted country. Far from being a "neutral observer" or a harbinger of social reform, the United States is a leading prop of apartheid.

Over 350 U.S. firms have investments in the neighborhood of $2.5 billion in the South African economy. In addition, U.S. banks have underwritten South Africa's apartheid policy with some $5 billion in loans. And U.S. firms have sold South Africa "non-military" items such as telecommunications hardware, computers, helicopters, arms, ammunition, etc., much of which supplements the arsenal of oppression and suppression that South Africa's state apparatus employs in its systematic enforcement of its apartheid policy.

To put it bluntly, apartheid in South Africa has long had the tacit approval and overt material support of U.S. capitalism. And it continues to have such support and approval despite hypocritical official statements that apartheid is "evil" and "totally repugnant" to the United States.

Facade of Reformism

For many years—including the years of the Carter administration—the official U.S. argument was that massive U.S. capital investments in South Africa would have a "reforming" impact on its apartheid policy. As then President Carter once put it: "I think our American businessman can be a constructive force for achieving racial justice in South Africa."

Carter probably knew better. By the time he came to office, the historic evidence was overwhelmingly to the contrary. For example, during the period from 1960 to 1975, U.S. investments in South Africa mushroomed from $280 million to over $1.6 billion. That same period saw the most ruthless consolidation of South Africa's apartheid system and the steadily worsening impoverishment of the black population.

Class rule has never been more than superficially concerned with tolerance, morality, equality or justice. But few ruling classes have succeeded in establishing for so long as complete and inexorable an apparatus of police-state control, brutal repression and vicious exploitation as South Africa's apartheid.

To maintain such a racist order requires constant surveillance and repeated acts to ruthlessly crush any effort to challenge apartheid or the social system—capitalism—upon which it rests. Accordingly, South Africa has erected one of the world's most repressive state machines. That machine not only serves to protect and maintain the privileges and wealth of the white ruling class, it also ensures the cheapest possible labor supply for both domestic capitalists and foreign multinationals.

Sechaba/LNS

Under the prevailing internal passport system, all blacks must carry racial identification passes. They are barred from entering "white-only" areas except to work. They are herded into barren "homelands" where women, children and surplus workers are forced to eke out a pitiful existence. Since 1960, 3.5 million blacks have been forcibly moved into designated tribal homelands. Some 8 million blacks have been stripped of South African citizenship by classifying them citizens of the homelands. In the past year alone, 160,000 blacks were arrested for acts against the pass laws.

Strikes by black workers are outlawed and they are barred from entering skilled jobs. Black workers' wages of only $60 to $140 a month enable U.S. firms to reap profits well above the world average.

Reaping the Benefits of Racism

Little wonder the U.S. capitalist class (and its political agents) stand firmly behind the racist South African government. They have reaped—and continue to reap—the benefits of racist exploitation.

The U.S. capitalists getting rich off black labor in Johannesburg and Salisbury are the same ones benefiting from racism in New York and Detroit. For this reason alone, it is important that U.S. workers stand with the oppressed workers of South Africa as they wage their difficult fight. It is not merely a matter of morality, or of altruism, or of humaneness, it is a matter of fundamental common interests—life and death interests.

146

Despite the jailing, torture and murder of blacks by South African police, protests continue to grow. In fact, as the forces of repression are augmented and officially sanctioned brutality is intensified, the resistance heightens. As one black observed, while unrest 25 or so years ago was "almost sporadic," today "unrest is endemic."

Though there is a sizable black proletariat in South Africa, the current struggles against apartheid have not taken on any distinct proletarian character. Nor does it aim at the capitalist system that sustains apartheid. Today, all forces are being mobilized for a basically national struggle against the white regime and its apartheid apparatus. As the struggle develops, however, class divisions will take on added importance. To the degree that working-class interests become predominant, to that extent the possibility will open up for transforming capitalist property relations as well as race relations.

The U.S. ruling class can be expected to do everything in its power to prevent this outcome. It is motivated, of course, by a concern to maintain its investments, access to raw materials, communications networks and control of vital shipping lanes around the Cape of Africa. Moreover, its counterrevolutionary instincts and interests are too well developed to permit it to do anything that would undermine the South African regime.

Socialist Internationalism

However, many U.S. workers and students do see the basic justice of the struggle against racial oppression as well as the fact that U.S. corporations are profiting from inhuman suffering. Many of those workers and students are expressing their opposition to apartheid and their solidarity with the South African struggle through protests and demonstrations.

Those protests and demonstrations offer the potential for building a mass movement that could politicize millions of workers throughout the country and awaken them not only to the realities of U.S. imperialism, but to the realities of capitalist society. Socialists working within the antiapartheid movement can widen its horizons and draw attention to the common class nature of the oppressors of workers in both South Africa and the United States. It can make the connection between imperialism abroad and capitalism at home, raise the banner of international proletarian solidarity, and expound the socialist road to freedom and security.

The struggle in South Africa will not put an end to all the oppression in the world. But that struggle is part of an international class struggle which, as Socialists, we believe must culminate in the overthrow of capitalism in the industrialized countries and the establishment of a world socialist order. Until that struggle is won, the system of class rule and the racism it breeds will remain international—so, too, must the resistance and solidarity of the workers of the world.

"Companies such as Control Data are among the real catalysts in the struggle for peaceful change [in South Africa]."

US Corporations Can Facilitate Change in South Africa

William C. Norris

William C. Norris is the former chairman and chief executive officer of Control Data Corporation. In the following viewpoint, Mr. Norris argues that US corporations have improved and continue to improve black human rights in South Africa. While condemning divestment, or the removal of all US corporations from South Africa, Mr. Norris argues for a system of selective divestment. Corporations who are actively working for changes in the apartheid system should be allowed to remain, while corporations that merely maintain the status quo should be made to leave.

As you read, consider the following questions:

1. Why does the author argue that US corporations should remain in South Africa?
2. What does the author suggest the US should do as an alternative to divestment?
3. What evidence does the author give that US corporations improve the lives of South African blacks?

William C. Norris, "South Africa: Let's Not Divest Blindly," *Los Angeles Times*, June 6, 1985. Reprinted with the author's permission.

While there can be no question about the need to stop the oppression of blacks, I do not believe that the politically convenient call for universal divestment is the best way of accomplishing that goal. Divestment might calm outspoken critics of discrimination, but there is little evidence that it would contribute to constructive change in South Africa.

What is needed is not just public outrage and emotional appeals for actions that may not take into account the complex realities of that troubled country. Indeed, total divestment might kill the best hope that the present generation of South African blacks has for economic opportunity by removing the powerful leverage for change that the U.S. business presence now exerts on their country's economy.

Catalysts for Change

Companies such as Control Data are among the real catalysts in the struggle for peaceful change. To declare these companies unworthy of...investments would be a step backward in the effort to build a more constructive relationship between the university and the business community. A much more effective approach is a strategy of selective investment: investing in U.S. companies committed to helping blacks attain full political and economic opportunity.

This is critically important, because even if apartheid were to end tomorrow, the majority of blacks in South Africa, having little or no education and training, would continue to be denied full access to economic opportunities.

Although selective investment would be harder to accomplish than universal divestment, it is attainable. At the same time, this selective-investment strategy could be coupled with faculty and student exchange programs with leading black South African and multiracial educational institutions. The result would be that the university would be not only teaching and learning but also helping to dismantle apartheid.

Only US Companies Are Concerned

Clearly, then, the implementation of a selective-investment strategy is crucial, because if U.S. institutions and businesses don't take a leadership role, it isn't likely to come from any other nations doing business in South Africa. Like most European companies, Japanese companies aren't showing much concern for the plight of black South Africans. Whenever a U.S. company is unable to export equipment to South Africa, Japanese companies snap up the business. Because of pressures for divestment and ever-changing U.S. export controls, South African customers are afraid to rely entirely on U.S. companies and are seeking alternatives, often in Tokyo. Our foreign competitors are eager to fuel such concerns. Even though Control Data's South African subsidiary represents less than 1% annually of our $5-billion worldwide revenues, we are committed to being at the forefront of U.S. corporations helping to improve education and training for South African blacks. At the same time we are working to accelerate the end of the morally repugnant apartheid system. We were among the first signatories of the Sullivan Principles, and assisted their author, the Rev. Leon Sullivan of Philadelphia, in gaining wider support for those principles as the most effective way of encouraging economic opportunity and social justice in South Africa.

At his request, I presented a concept for an extensive education and job-creation program for South African blacks to a group of executives representing European, South African and U.S. corporations at a meeting in England. The planning and direction of such an effort would be provided by an international consortium made up of corporations doing business in South Africa, and other organizations such as churches and foundations.

Don't Divest!

A survey by South Africa's foremost analyst of poll data, Lawrence Schlemmer, reveals that more than 75 percent of black workers surveyed oppose disvestment as a strategy to liberate them because they fear that it would destroy the jobs on which their lives and families depend....

Although 60 percent of the workers polled said that their condition was deteriorating, the majority said that they preferred the free-enterprise system over socialism, and most said that American companies exerted a constructive pressure for better jobs and working conditions.

Dinesh D'Souza, *The New York Times*, August 20, 1985.

While it is too early to say whether the concept will be implemented, there is no question that it could be. The plan is based on proven methodology, and provides a vehicle for those who really want to help. It is a constructive alternative to advocating measures that will only force U.S. companies to leave South Africa, thereby denying blacks help from one of their important allies.

Improving Life

The presence of Control Data and most other U.S. companies in South Africa has been, and continues to be, a significant force for improving life for black South Africans, which, more than anything, will help ultimately to end apartheid. Many of the products and services that we have developed—particularly computer-based education and training— are targeted specifically at improving the access of black South Africans to better education and economic opportunity.

"Capitalism itself...[is] being increasingly questioned—the very efforts of corporations and the United States government to 'sell' capitalism through advertising is indication of such questioning."

Capitalism Destroyed the Latin American Economy

Phillip Berryman

Phillip Berryman is a writer who began working in Central America in 1965 researching the role of the Catholic Church in Latin America. From 1976 to 1980, while a Central American representative for the American Friends Service Committee, he was in a position to observe the deepening crisis in the region. He returned to the US from Guatemala in 1980 and has since published numerous articles in leading Christian journals and a book, *The Religious Roots of Rebellion*, from which this viewpoint is excerpted. In the viewpoint, he uses the example of the running of a coffee plantation to explain how capitalist modes of production create massive poverty in Latin America.

As you read, consider the following questions:

1. How is the Latin American economy geared to service world interests, not its own interests, according to the author?
2. The author makes an argument for "expropriation," or seizing privately-owned lands and redistributing them. Why does he see this as a necessity?

Phillip Berryman, *The Religious Roots of Rebellion*. Maryknoll, New York: Orbis Books, 1984. Reprinted with permission.

I would like to start...with an examination of what may at first seem to be simply an example, but which I believe will lead to the heart of the question: the functioning of a *finca*, or agroexport plantation.

Let us picture a coffee plantation in the foothills of the mountains of Guatemala (the example could equally well be a sugar or cotton plantation and be in El Salvador or Nicaragua). Coffee production requires considerable expertise and skill for best results: seedlings and plants do not begin to produce until after four years and then attention must be paid to pruning the shade trees carefully, weeding, spraying, vigilance for disease. The day-to-day management is under the care of an administrator and supervisors. Labor is done on a piecework basis. For much of the year little labor is needed and is performed by a small permanent crew and additional, hired day laborers. During harvest time (August-December, varying by altitude) large labor gangs are contracted.

The owner does not live on the plantation but in the capital city because of its better climate, schools for his children, amenities, and social contacts. Moreover, by leaving daily management to the administrator the owner can engage in other businesses, investing profits from the plantation. Basic decisions about the plantation (new investment, financing) and particularly about selling (futures) can best be made from the capital.

Profitability of a Plantation

Let us examine the profitability of such a plantation, using rounded figures (duly making some qualifications). If annual production is 5,000 one-hundred-pound sacks, production costs are $50 per sack, market price is $200 per sack, and the government taxes sales above $50 per sack at 45 percent, the result is the following:

Production cost (labor and inputs) ($50 x 5,000)	$250,000
Export tax (.45 x 750,000)	337,500
Post-tax profit	412,500
Total	$1,000,000

These simplified figures will require some nuancing, but first I would point to the relative rewards to labor and capital in coffee production. The largest single amount of labor per unit is the hand-picking done during harvest time by Indians, who come down from the highlands. Prior to the 1980 raise in the minimum wage, people would get perhaps $1.75 for picking 100 pounds of coffee beans (roughly a day's work, although some could pick more). Since it would take two-and-a-half bags of picked beans to make 100 pounds of processed and dried beans ready for export, the harvest labor in our example would be $4.37 per bag. This means that the two-and-a-half days of bean-by-bean picking amounted to less than one-tenth of the total production cost and received less than 2.5 percent of the price paid for the coffee on the international market. There were, of course, other labor costs including the care given the seedling and young plant before it became productive, spraying, weeding, and so forth, as well as the processing (which, except for sorting the beans, is largely done by machines).

A plantation producing 5,000 bags of coffee in Guatemala is large, but not the largest: one-third of the coffee comes from fewer than 80 plantations that produce 6,000 bags or more....

It...seems clear that a small group of people, the plantation owners, receive great profits while those who do the actual work receive a pittance. Certainly the owners assume the risks of bad weather, insects, and disease (minimized through insurance) and fluctuating prices (which can be passed on to commodities traders or exporters). Plantation owners like to speak of themselves as "producers," meaning that they bring together the "factors of production" (labor, inputs, and management), but they are rewarded in a manner far disproportionate to their real contribution.

Capitalist Plunder

U.S. capitalist investments in lesser developed countries actually help impoverish those countries rather than help develop their economies.

Agribusiness corporations help throw peasants off the land, swelling the ranks of the unemployed. Resource wealth and profits are taken out of these countries and do nothing to help develop them. The countries are kept in perpetual debt by the control of their economies by U.S. industry, the fostered reliance on U.S. imports, and loan-sharking-type banking practices.

In sum, Central America is being plundered, not developed, by U.S. capitalism.

The People, August 18, 1984.

Let us take this case from the local level, the plantation, to the country as a whole. In Guatemala 55 percent of the coffee production is in the hands of some 300 enterprises. It is reasonable to assume that these represent approximately 300 families (although some plantations are jointly owned, some families own or have shares in more than one plantation). Taking into account the extreme fluctuations of coffee prices, it is safe to say that each of these families receives hundreds of thousands of dollars—and some receive millions—a year. For the most part this same group is dominant in other kinds of plantations (cotton, sugar, beef, and some new crops) and in business and industry.

This ownership leads to extreme disparity of income: according to the United States embassy in Guatemala, the top 2 percent of the population receives 25 percent of the income, while the bottom 50 percent receives from 10 to 15 percent. If we average the last figure at 12.5 percent, the top 2 percent then receives as a group double the total income of the bottom half. In other words, individuals and families of the *upper 2 percent* enjoy *fifty times* the income of the *bottom half* of the population.

In some regions of the world such disparities might reflect a "dual economy": "backward" peoples living alongside "advanced" groups. However, the whole point of what we have been saying is that it is the *labor* of that bottom half (largely Indians) that produces the *wealth*, which is then divided unevenly. The *poverty* of Indians in the highlands with too little land is *functional*: it makes them available as a cheap, seasonal labor supply in the agroexport areas. The human results are well known: children are continually undernourished, many die in their first year or early years, families are chronically in debt, children have little schooling and few opportunities, there is little health care.

In addition, there is another effect somewhat more abstract, but important to consider. Not only do the profits accrue to a small class of people; the economy as a whole functions not to meet the basic needs of its people but to supply a series of tropical products to the world market. A clear indication is that while land for export crops in Guatemala increased dramatically after World War II, that devoted to basic foods did not keep up with the population. Thus the economy is distorted by its agroexport function....

Growing Gap Between Rich and Poor

At Puebla the Latin American bishops called the growing gap between rich and poor a "scandal and contradiction to Christian existence," saying that it was "the product of economic, social, and political situations and structures" and calling for "personal conversion and profound structural changes." Puebla was simply repeating and summarizing what had been stated repeatedly by individual conferences and bishops.

Disagreement begins, however, as soon as the question is raised of how this structural change is to take place. The conventional answer is "development": premature efforts to redistribute wealth in a poor society would simply inhibit growth and make everyone poorer. However, Central America has experienced two or three decades of "development": infrastructures (roads, energy, and water systems) have been built, new industries have been created through the incentives of the Central American Common Market, governments have made development plans, technology and managerial expertise has been transferred. In the late 1960s and

154

early 1970s when it was clear that not enough was "trickling down" to give the poor any substantial benefits, international agencies and some governments began to "target" the "bottom 40 percent" with programs directly aimed at improving their welfare (cooperatives, improved agricultural techniques, marketing, health and education services). These programs, in Central America at least, have ship-wrecked on the hard rock of economic reality: Central American economies require a cheap labor supply of people who are landless or nearly landless; no "development" threatening that requirement can be permitted, and yet such a group of people can never con-stitute a market that will stimulate investment to serve its needs. Thus there is an inbuilt structural tendency toward extreme disparities of wealth and poverty, and indeed, pauperization.

Capitalism or Feudalism?

Some people, sensing an anticapitalist thrust to the present argu-ment, might say, "The problem in Central America is not capitalism but feudalism. The kind of economy you are describing is back-ward. What you need is not less capitalism but more, the kind that will develop the daring, creativity, dynamism, and ingenuity of entrepreneurs and enkindle hope in a people who see a chance for their betterment."

Capitalism a Threat

Many Central Americans have increasingly associated capitalism with a brutal oligarchy-military complex that has been supported by U.S. policies—and armies. Capitalism, as they see it, has too often threatened the survival of many for the sake of freedom for a few.

Walter LaFeber, *Inevitable Revolutions: The United States in Central America,* 1983.

This, however, is a loose use of the term "feudal," making it more or less synonymous with "backwardness." Central American economies are not feudal, since the landowner, unlike the medieval lord, has no obligation to the workers (to provide protection, or food in times of famine). Their relationship is thoroughly capitalist in that the owner of the means of production (the plantation) buys the labor power of the workers, who are economically forced to sell it. The overall tendency is proletarization: more and more people are without the least means of production (small plots of land). While this may be "underdeveloped capitalism," it is capitalism nevertheless.

Moreover, there is no built-in tendency for it to evolve in a direc-tion in which the basic contradictions will be resolved. The reason is simple and obvious: the oligarchies, in league with the military, manage the political process and have been willing to support a

155

high degree of repression to maintain their privilege. El Salvador's frustrated "land reforms" are eloquent proof.

For our present purposes, the question is not "capitalism" as a whole but the Central American economies, which are capitalist. It is evident, however, that capitalism itself (and not simply "abuses" associated with it) are being increasingly questioned— the very efforts of corporations and the United States government to "sell" capitalism through advertising is indication of such questioning. While I have no intention of contributing any real substance to the debate, I would simply note that it often tends to be unhistorical and static, that is, the question is stated as "capitalism vs. socialism." However, capitalism is not an eternal essence but a phenomenon in history: as a system it began during the eighteenth century, although elements of it had appeared before. As a phenomenon in history it is either some kind of definitive achievement of the human race, destined to remain forever or—more likely—it is a stage destined to give way to something else. It is the contention of many that the seeds of this "something else" are already present and can be seen in the "contradictions" of capitalism, and that the new form will be called "socialism," since the main means of production will be socially owned and managed. Its convinced defenders might argue that whereas in principle capitalism may eventually be superseded by new forms, they are as yet unforeseeable and the question is irrelevant. However, a growing number see the question as indeed relevant and critical for understanding what is happening in our age. This historical angle on the question helps illuminate the objection that "socialism" has failed: socialism has a much shorter history and existing examples may be seen as initial efforts, partial successes, or even false starts toward the "something else" to which capitalism will give way.

What I mean to say with the preceding excursus is that the present discussion on Central America may be seen in two ways. For some it is simply a manifestation of a larger crisis of the capitalist system; for others it may be viewed as a special and extreme case, which may call for extraordinary responses. I would hope that even those who see no need to question capitalism in principle will give some consideration to my present argument.

Structural Changes Needed

To return to the basic question of "what is to be done," I would assert that the "structural changes" needed involve changing the functioning of the economy so that the main means of production (plantations, factories) serve the people in such a way that:

1. the workers receive a fair share of the wealth they produce
2. profits are reinvested for true development rather than serving the further aggrandizement or luxury consumption of elites

156

3. production is aimed at the basic needs of the majority: (a) food self-sufficiency, and (b) basic consumer items for all (clothing, shoes, household items, and so forth)
4. essential social services (schooling and health care) are provided
5. workers are involved in management rather than simply being factors of production

Such a course would necessitate a considerable amount of direct expropriation. While expropriation might strike some as unjust—to the degree that they hold property rights to be absolute (or a kind of "first principle")—I would argue that in the case of Central American oligarchies *justice demands expropriation*, and I wish to state this proposition in its most direct and possibly offensive form before considering possible qualifications.

First, the real development of the poor is incompatible with such extreme division not only of wealth, but of income and power. There simply will be no development for the poor in Guatemala, for example, as long as the top 2 percent as a group receives double the income of the lower half of the population.

Second, the wealth of the oligarchy is not primarily the result of entrepreneurial genius, but, rather, the product of an original expropriation (lands taken from the Indians and the church in the 1870s) and continuing exploitation (for example, in Nebaj, Guatemala, all the local landholding elites began their fortunes as labor contractors). Not all are subjectively guilty, of course. Today's families have often simply inherited wealth and consider it "natural" that they should enjoy privilege. Some people of middle-class origins studied, became professionals, saved, and bought agroexport property. However, the agroexport system remains objectively exploitive, independent of the intentions of the owners.

Wealth Leaves Latin America

Third, Central American oligarchies have already taken vast sums of their wealth out of their countries. While Swiss bank accounts were traditional, the movement in recent years is astounding. Somoza and his associates took an amount equivalent to 96 percent of one year's GNP (gross national product); figures for El Salvador are imprecise, but it seems that a similar amount may have been removed. That a tiny elite should be able to remove in dollars an amount equivalent to the value of a whole year's production of goods and services in the entire country is another striking example of their economic power. It also lessens concern for their fate in the case of expropriation.

To repeat: in my view, a broad expropriation of the means of production from the hands of the oligarchies in order to restructure the economy to serve the needs of the poor would not only *not* be unjust, but would, on the contrary, be an act of justice.

"It is odd, on the face of it, to blame the poverty of the rest of the world on democratic capitalism. Such poverty, after all, is hundreds of years older than its purported cause."

Capitalism Aided Latin America

Michael Novak

Michael Novak is Resident Scholar in philosophy, religion and public policy at the American Enterprise Institute in Washington, DC. He has published several influential books including *Belief and Unbelief, The Rise of the Unmeltable Ethnics*, and *The Spirit of Democratic Capitalism*, from which this viewpoint is excerpted. In the viewpoint, Mr. Novak offers several reasons why capitalism aided Latin America, and how the present trend toward socialism is ruining it.

As you read, consider the following questions:

1. What is the attraction of socialism in Latin America, according to the author?
2. Why is the idea that US investment ruined economic opportunity "preposterous," according to the author?
3. Why does the author believe that Catholicism is to blame for Latin American poverty?

> The principal guilt for the economic dependence of our countries rests with powers *inspired* by uncontrolled desire for gain, which leads to economic dictatorship and "the international imperialism of money"....
>
> —Conference of Latin American Bishops, Medillín, 1968

On few continents of the planet is the socialist myth more vigorous than in Latin America, where it seems well suited to the political culture, if badly suited to the moral culture, of traditional societies. The vision of socialism legitimates an authoritarian (even a totalitarian) order. It ensures order and stability. In Cuba and Nicaragua, it permits the abrogation of elections and the suppression of dissent. It legitimates the wholesale indoctrination of populations in a millenarian vision. It unites the political system, the economic system, and the moral-cultural system under one set of authorities. It now inspires the most heavily armed states on the continent.

Yet one attraction of socialism may also be that it provides an excuse. Confronting the relatively inferior economic performance of their continent, the Catholic bishops of Latin America do not now blame themselves for the teachings about political economy which Latin American Catholicism has nourished for four hundred years. Conveniently, socialist theory allows them to blame the United States and other successful economic powers. No passion better fits the fundamental Marxist stencil, which offers a universally applicable paradigm: *If I am poor, my poverty is due to malevolent and powerful others.*

Capitalism and Poverty

The use of this stencil illustrates a transformation in socialist theory. Whereas Marx based the promise of socialism upon the predicted failures of democratic capitalism, the new socialists attack its successes, to which they attribute their own failures. Democratic capitalism, they say, is responsible for the poverty of the Third World. It typically creates a "center" which oppresses "the periphery," offers reform and development which either don't work or take too long, imposes unfavorable terms of trade on Third World nations, and acts through multinational corporations which are outside the law. Nearly all these accusations are alluded to in the statement of the Latin American episcopate meeting at Medellin in 1968:

> Another feature of this economic situation is our subjection to capital interests in foreign lands. In many cases, these foreign interests exercise unchecked control, their power continues to grow, and they have no permanent interest in the countries of Latin America. Moreover, Latin American trade is jeopardized by its heavy dependence on the developed countries. They buy raw materials from Latin America at a cheap price, and then sell manufactured products to Latin America at ever higher prices; and these manufactured goods are necessary for Latin America's

continuing development.

We ought to weigh these accusations.

It is odd, on the face of it, to blame the poverty of the rest of the world on democratic capitalism. Such poverty, after all, is hundreds of years older than its purported cause. Two hundred years ago, Latin America was poorer than it is today; but so was North America. At that time, Adam Smith drew attention to the two contrasting experiments taking place in "the New World," one on the southern continent and one on the northern, one based on the political economy of southern Europe, the other launching a new idea.

Churches Stole the Wealth

In those early days, Latin America seemed to have greater physical resources than North America. Much of its gold, silver, and lead ended up in the ornate churches and chapels of the Catholic church in Spain and Portugal. Columbus himself, seeking gold and other precious resources, sailed under a Spanish flag. By contrast, the first settlers in New England discovered a relatively harsh agricultural environment. Such riches as they won from North America consisted of tobacco, furs, corn, and later cotton, which they traded to Europe for manufactured goods.

In 1800, there were about 4 million European settlers in the United States, about 900,000 blacks, and an estimated 1 million "Indians." The population of South America was then three times larger, numbering 19 million, of which the original population of Indians, estimated at between 25 and 50 million in 1500, had been dramatically reduced. By 1940, the populations of the United States and Latin America were about equal, some 130 million each. By 1977, the population of the United States had reached a relatively stable 220 million but that of Latin America had shot up to 342 million.

In computing average per capita income, population is important in three ways. First, every newborn child lowers the average per capita income. Second, as the cohorts of those under age eighteen increase in proportion, the relative number of productive workers decreases. Third, rapidly increasing populations indicate that many parents have decided in favor of larger families, through whatever combination of motives. This is an admirable preference. But it has, in some but not all respects, economic costs. Those who make that choice cannot properly blame others for its consequences. Since 1940, the population of the United States has grown by 90 million, that of Latin America by 210 million.

In the nineteenth century, on both continents, independence was relatively new. Both had recently been colonies of the then greatest powers in Europe. All through the nineteenth century, trade between Latin America and North America was negligible. Nearly all trade between either continent was transatlantic trade with Europe.

In North America, the vast majority of persons became owners of their homes and lands; not so in Latin America. The moral-cultural system of North America placed great emphasis on building and working for tomorrow. The moral-cultural system of Latin America favored other values. . . .

Consider what might have been. Suppose that Latin America had developed industries and manufacturing before the United States did. Clearly, the resources were available. Latin America is rich in oil, tin, bauxite, and many other important minerals. Its farmlands and tropical gardens are luxuriant. Why, then, didn't Latin America become the richer of the two continents of the New World? The answer appears to lie in the quite different nature of the Latin American political system, economic system, and moral-cultural system. The last is probably decisive. Latin America might have been economically active, progressive, and independent. Indeed, Latin America had the advantage of remaining outside World Wars I and II. It might long ago have placed the United States in its economic shadow. It might yet do so, if it were to organize itself to use its own great wealth in an appropriate way. Yet its Catholic bishops do not blame the Catholic church, the systems of political economy they long supported, or the past values and choices of its peoples. They blame the United States.

Dependence on the US?

Specific emphasis is placed upon practices of trade. During the nineteenth century, trade between Latin America and the United States was minimal. Between 1900 and 1950, trade did begin to grow, but by 1950 the total historical investment of U.S. companies in Latin America totaled only $4.6 billion. During World War II, Western Europe lay in rubble, its economies broken, and Japan lay economically prostrate. After the war, trade between the United States and Latin America grew. Still, by 1965, the total value of all U.S. investments in Latin America was $11 billion. By 1965, investments by Western European nations and Japan, just beginning to revive after World War II, were not of great significance. It seems preposterous to believe that such small sums are responsible for the poverty or the dependence of Latin America. They are neither a high proportion of the wealth of the investing nations nor a high proportion of Latin America's internally generated wealth. The total U.S. investment of $11 billion averages out to $44 per capita for the 250 million Latin Americans of 1965. Moreover, U.S. investments in Western Europe and Japan during that same period were many times higher, without producing similar "dependence." Is it supposed that such investments in Latin America should have been forbidden altogether?

Traditional Catholic ignorance about modern economics may, in fact, have more to do with the poverty of Latin America than any other single factor.

Distinguishing Between Fact and Opinion

This activity is designed to help develop the basic reading and thinking skill of distinguishing between fact and opinion. Consider the following statement as an example: "Control Data's South African subsidiary represents less than 1% annually of its $5 billion worldwide revenues." This statement is a fact which can be proved by checking the corporate reports. But consider another statement concerning this company's investments in South Africa: "The presence of Control Data and most other U.S. companies in South Africa is a significant force for improving life for black South Africans, which, more than anything, will help ultimately to end apartheid." This statement uses the fact of the company's presence in a foreign country to assume a conclusion which cannot be substantiated.

When investigating controversial issues it is important that one be able to distinguish between statements of fact and statements of opinion. It is also important to recognize that not all statements of fact are true. They may appear to be true, but some are based on inaccurate or false information. For this activity, however, we are concerned with understanding the difference between those statements which appear to be factual and those which appear to be based primarily on opinion.

Most of the following statements are taken from the viewpoints in this chapter. Consider each statement carefully. *Mark O for any statement you believe is an opinion or interpretation of facts. Mark F for any statement you believe is a fact.*

If you are doing this activity as a member of a class or group, compare your answers with those of other class or group members. Be able to defend your answers. You may discover that others will come to different conclusions than you. Listening to the reasons others present for their answers may give you valuable insights in distinguishing between fact and opinion.

If you are reading this book alone, ask others if they agree with your answers. You too will find this interaction very valuable.

O = opinion
F = fact

1. Democratic capitalism has generated more development, more innovation, and more wealth than all other systems combined have produced in the history of mankind.

2. Democratic capitalism is the Third World's greatest hope for sustainable economic development.

3. In the Soviet Union agricultural productivity on the private plots citizens are permitted to farm in their spare time is thirty times the productivity of the state-run collective farms.

4. In terms of human capital and economic systems, most developing countries are many decades behind the West.

5. There are people in the US who count themselves poor because they live with a black and white TV, a six-year-old car and a weekly rent obligation.

6. By its nature democratic capitalism has heaped more wealth on some individuals and countries than on others.

7. Juárez, Mexico is home to about 125 foreign-owned factories that employ 45,000 people—a manufacturing center larger than Youngstown, Ohio.

8. Labor costs in Mexico generally run 20 to 25 percent of what they would be in the US; the work week is 25 percent longer and the pace of work is faster.

9. Mexican workers near the border spend between a third and a half of their earnings on the US side.

10. In Juárez a "surplus" population of people lives in cardboard shacks and feeds its young by begging or selling items scavenged from American parks, alleys, and dumps.

11. The movement of Mexican women into American border factories has strained traditional sex roles.

12. Apartheid in South Africa has long had the tacit approval and covert material support of US capitalism.

13. Over 350 US firms have investments in the neighborhood of $2.5 billion in the South African economy.

14. Class rule has never been more than superficially concerned with tolerance, morality, equality or justice.

15. South Africa has erected one of the world's most repressive state machines.

16. Black workers' wages in South Africa of only $60 to $140 a month enable US firms to reap profits well above the world average.

Bibliography

The following bibliography deals with the subject matter of this chapter.

Phillip Berryman	*The Religious Roots of Rebellion.* Maryknoll, NY: Orbis Books, 1984.
Dan Dickinson	"Capitalism in the Third World," *Conservative Digest*, April 1984.
Dan Dickinson	"Free Enterprise: The Salvation of Many Third World Countries," *Human Events*, January 21, 1984.
engage/social action	"Conglomerates: Where the Product Is Profit," November 1984.
Milton Friedman	*Capitalism and Freedom.* Chicago and London: The University of Chicago Press, 1982.
Pranay Gupte	"Third World Success Story," *Forbes*, June 18, 1984.
Walter LaFeber	*Inevitable Revolutions: The United States in Central America.* New York: W.W. Norton, 1983.
Robert Lehrman	"How Business Can Chip at Apartheid," *The New York Times*, September 9, 1985.
Herbert McCloskey and John Zaller	*The American Ethos: Public Attitudes Toward Capitalism & Democracy.* Cambridge, MA: Harvard University Press, 1984.
Frank Morris	"Capitalism Can Be Reformed, Marxism Cannot," *The Wanderer*, October 4, 1984.
Michael Novak	*The Spirit of Democratic Capitalism.* New York: Simon & Schuster, 1982.
Marvin Ott	"Asia and Africa Are Increasingly Open to U.S. Overtures," *Los Angeles Times*, July 16, 1985.
The People	"Upsurge in Class Struggle Shakes South Africa Regime," August 17, 1985.
Cal Thomas	"World's Starving Need Capitalism, Not Charity," *St. Paul Pioneer Press and Dispatch*, October 28, 1985.
Richard S. Williamson	"Third World Needs Free Economies," *Human Events*, October 20, 1984.

Index